CANADIAN WARSHIPS

· SINCE 1956 ·

CANADIAN WARSHIPS
SINCE 1956

Roger G. Steed

Vanwell Publishing Limited
ST. CATHARINES, ONTARIO

Cover: HMCS *Halifax* launches a Harpoon surface-to-surface missile. The two missile racks, each capable of holding four missiles, are mounted athwartships, at a 35° angle to the deck, pointing to port and to starboard. The *Halifax* is the first of 12 Canadian Patrol Frigates (CPF). This view clearly shows her fully enclosed bridge and her Bofors 57-mm L/70 Mk 2 rapid firing, dual-purpose gun mounting, designed to deal with air and surface targets. (Photo courtesy DND)

Vanwell Publishing Limited
1 Northrup Crescent, Box 2131
St. Catharines, ON L2R 7S2

Copyright 1999 by Roger G. Steed. All rights reserved. No part of this publication may be reproduced, stored in a retrieval system, or transmitted in any form without the written permission of the publisher.

We acknowledge the financial support of the Government of Canada through the Book Publishing Industry Development Program for our publishing activities.

Canadian Cataloguing in Publication Data

Steed, Roger G.
 Canadian warships since 1956

Includes bibliographical references and index
ISBN 1-55125-025-X

1. Canada. Royal Canadian Navy - List of vessels. 2. Warships - Canada History - 20th century - Pictorial works. I. Title.

VA400.S73 1999   359.8'35'0971   C99-930485-2

Canadian Warships

TABLE OF CONTENTS

v	Foreword
vi	Acknowledgements
vii	Introduction
9	HMCS *Bonaventure*
10	*Bonaventure* fuelling *Chaudiére*
11	HMCS *Ontario*
12	HMCS *Ontario*
13	HMCS *Québec*
14	HMCS *Sioux* and HMCS *Crusader*
15	HMCS *Athabaskan* (2nd)
16	HMCS *Athabaskan* (2nd)
17	HMC Dockyard, Halifax
18	Radar Frequency Bands
19	HMCS *Algonquin* (1st)
20	HMCS *Algonquin* (1st) and Argus aircraft
21	HMCS *Algonquin* (1st) Limbo Armament
22	HMCS *Algonquin* (1st)
23	HMCS *Crescent*
24	HMCS *Stettler*
25	Two Bird's-eye Views of HMCS *Sussexvale*
26	HMCS *Beacon Hill* in Jackstay Transfer with *Sussexvale*
27	Two Close-up Views of *Stettler*
29	HMCS *St. Laurent*, as Originally Built
30	*St. Laurent* as a DDH
31	HMCS *Gatineau* as Originally Built
32	The *Restigouche* Class Bow
33	On HMCS *Chaudiére's* Bridge
34	*Restigouche* Class's Original Mast
34	Modern Marine Radars
35	HMCS *Terra Nova*
36	The Hydrofoil HMCS *Bras d'Or*
37	Improved *Restigouche* Class in Harbour
38	HMCS *Provider* Fuelling USS *Ticonderoga*
39	HMCS *Provider* Fuelling *Algonquin*
40	HMCS *Saskatchewan*
41	HMCS *Annapolis* Berthed on *Provider*
42	Squid and Limbo
43	HMCS *Terra Nova* in Later Life
44	HMCS *Gatineau* and *Terra Nova* at Extended Readiness
45	*Gatineau's* Bridge and Mast
46	*Gatineau's* Superstructure
47	HMCS *Assiniboine's* Variable Depth Sonar
48	A Variable Depth Sonar Drogue
49	Sea King Helicopter and Bear Trap
50	The Later *Tribals*: HMCS *Iroquois* (2nd)
51	*Iroquois* as Originally Built
52	HMCS *Iroquois*
54	Sea King Haul-Down
55	HMCS *Iroquois*, TRUMPed
56	*Iroquois* in Saint John Harbour
57	HMCS *Ville de Québec*: the *Halifax* Class CPF
58	HMCS *Ville de Québec*
59	HMCS *Toronto*
60	The *Halifax* Class; A Modern Warship
63	HMCS *Preserver* and *Iroquois*
64	HMCSm *Grilse*
65	HMCSm *Rainbow*
66	HMCSm *Okanagan* and HMCSm *Ojibwa*
67	The Royal Navy's Upholder Class
68	HMCS *Yukon* and the Minesweepers
69	HMCS *Chignecto*
70	HMCS *Cape Breton*
71	HMCS *Anticosti* and HMCS *Porte St. Jean*
72	HMCS *Kingston*
73	HMCS *Cormorant*
74	Yard Auxiliary Gate Vessels
75	HMCS *Cape Breton*, HMCS *Restigouche* & HMCS *Kootenay*

Appendix

78	Appendix A: Ships by Class, with Hull Numbers, Builders and Key Dates
81	Appendix B: Recollections of Command of Three Ships, by Vice Admiral J.A. Fulton Ret'd
82	Appendix C: An Officer-of-the-Watch's Impression of Driving a *Halifax* Class CPF, by Slt G. R. Steed
84	Appendix D: Astro Navigation: An Explanation
85	Appendix E: Anchoring a Warship: It's More Than Just Dropping the Hook!
86	Appendix F: Ordering Engine Movements, and Steam Turbine Propulsion
88	Appendix G: Gas Turbine Marine Propulsion
91	Bibliography
92	Index

FOREWORD

All ships, but most particularly naval vessels, with their inherent grace and functional lines, are natural subjects for the photographer's art. Proof lies in this splendid collection of images of Canadian Navy ships spanning the last 42 years of the more than half-century from World War Two to the present. The many thousands of officers, men and women who served in these ships will be touched with nostalgia and a good deal of pride in reading this book, and others with an interest in Canada's navy will find it not only entertaining but an excellent source of technical and operational information on the "Senior Service". Regrettably, one is struck by the diminution in size of the navy during this time, but this is ameliorated somewhat by the steady improvements in capability culminating in the latest class of patrol frigate so excitingly described in the later chapters. These splendid vessels with the latest in electronics, propulsion and weapon technology, are equal to any of their class in the world. Roger Steed is to be congratulated in bringing together in this tightly organized volume the visually stimulating essence of the post war evolution of the surface navy.

Admiral (Ret'd) Robert H. Falls, CMM, CD, NDC, CF

Acknowledgements

Unless otherwise noted, the photographs are the author's. However, I have used several taken by my son, Sub-Lieutenant Geoffrey Steed, as well as several Department of National Defence (DND) photographs to augment my own collection. Vice-Admiral J.A. Fulton (Ret'd), my former commanding officer in *Gatineau*, very kindly let me browse through his collection of photographs, and choose whatever I liked. I have included three of them. He kindly contributed the note in Appendix B. Cdr Laverne Fleck, a former commanding officer of *Toronto*, generously contributed the article titled "Halifax Class: A Modern Warship", and my son wrote the piece in Appendix C.

I must also gratefully acknowledge making considerable use of *The Ships of Canada's Naval Forces 1910-1993*, by Ken Macpherson and John Burgess, an excellent reference work covering all Canadian warships, which I highly recommend to the reader. Unfortunately, I could only obtain two suitable pictures of *Quebec* from DND to include in this book, and the better one of them is already in Macpherson's and Burgess' book. I have also quoted from, and taken information from, *Jane's Fighting Ships*, the standard reference work for all the world's navies and warships. In addition, I have included data from the Canadian Navy's Maritime Command Internet Web Site. Sandy McClearn's *Canadian Navy of Yesterday and Today* Internet Web Site has also been of considerable help. Sandy very kindly answered quite a few questions.

Several people have assisted in tracking down information and photographs: Marilyn Gurney, curator of the Maritime Command Museum, sent several photographs; Barbara Trenholm of the Defence Research Establishment Atlantic, sent the photograph of *Bras d'Or*; George W. Kimball of Raytheon, answered questions about various radars; Brett Mitchell of the Royal Australian Navy's Directorate of Public Information answered questions about the loss of HMAS *Voyager*, and sent me a copy of the report of the commission of inquiry; Janet LaCroix of the Canadian Forces Photo Unit in Ottawa hunted down many photographs of various ships which I needed, and sent photocopies from which I could choose which to order; LCdr Glenn Chamberlain sent several photographs, and helped me get in touch with the commanding officers of the Canadian Forces Naval Operations and Engineering Schools; Cdr P.A. Guindon, Commandant of the Canadian Forces Naval Operations School, passed on my request for information the school no longer held to the Maritime Command Museum. Lt(N) C.E. Henderson, Base Public Affairs Officer, CFB Esquimalt, obtained detailed information about the YAGs. Cdr R.W. Greenwood, Commandant of the Canadian Forces Naval Engineering School sent detailed information concerning the machinery of the DDEs, and Donald Kerr, of Saint John Shipbuilding, directed me to Hugh Simpson, Information Manager, Canadian Patrol Frigate Project, who obtained the photograph of the *Toronto* steaming in rough seas. The photograph of the four *Upholder* class submarines was provided by the Royal Navy's Photographic Section, following up the lead of Ken Johnston, Senior Press Officer, and is British Crown Copyright/MOD. It is reproduced with the permission of the Controller of Her Britannic Majesty's Stationery Office. Wayne Sefcik, of Sigma Signals Corporation, directed me to *The Antenna Engineering Handbook*, in a hunt for radar frequency bands. Lts. Gerry Pash and David McKinnon, of Navy Public Affairs, obtained decommissioning dates and assisted with identifying ships in some recent photographs. Hugh Plant, of the Artificial Reef Society of Nova Scotia, and a former CO of *Fraser*, gave information about his plans for preserving this DDH. C.M. (Mike) Olsen, of General Electric International, Inc., Marine Engines, provided detailed information about the LM2500 Gas Turbine.

I should like to thank Angela Dobler, Vanwell Publishing's editor, and also Jeff Hardy of Caters Hardy Creative Design for the very pleasing final design. Finally, I must recognize my wife and family's long-suffering patience in tolerating my constant preoccupation with this book over the last two and a half years, and my son Geoffrey's help in answering my questions, while being careful not to divulge classified information. I affectionately dedicate this book to them.

Introduction

Canada's Navy since the end of the Second World War has included a varied assortment of ships ranging from aircraft carriers and light cruisers all the way down to wooden minesweepers and patrol craft. This work includes photographs of the major warships and views of representative members of the classes of smaller ships, attempting to show as much detail as possible. I have in general organized the photographs in order of decreasing size and age of ship, newest and/or smallest last. In a short work, such as this, it is not practicable to include photographs of every ship, or even every class of ship, and I apologize in advance for not including a shot of the ship in which you may have served.

As a naval cadet and junior officer, I enjoyed taking photographs of ships, and this book shows some of them. Living now in Saint John, New Brunswick, has presented several opportunities to photograph warships when they have visited the city. My son is now a junior naval officer, and he also enjoys taking shots of naval subjects whenever possible. Several of his photographs have made worthwhile additions to this book.

When I first suggested the idea of this book to a friend, he was quick to point out that it should not be a mini *Jane's Fighting Ships*. However, upon reflection, one has to recognize that many readers do not have easy access to that marvellous reference work, either in their local library or on their own bookshelves. Apart from that, *Jane's* shows all the warships of all the world's navies at an essentially single point in time in an annually issued volume, whereas this work is attempting to give an impression, in a fair amount of detail, of only Canadian warships which have been operational over a 42-year period, a quite different objective. Some of the information presented herein will, admittedly be found in *Jane's*, and in fact has been taken from *Jane's,* and must be included in a work purporting to deal with warships.

Roger G. Steed
Saint John, NB
April, 1999

HMCS Bonaventure

This photograph of HMCS *Bonaventure* was taken from *Chaudière* as the latter was breaking away, having fuelled from "Bonnie" in the western north Atlantic in June 1963. Two of the Bonnie's anti-submarine Tracker aircraft are parked with their wings folded on the forward flight deck, and "Pedro", her faithful HU-21 HO4S-3 helicopter, is parked aft.

Bonaventure was Canada's fifth and last aircraft carrier, having been preceded by two converted merchantmen, HMS *Nabob* and HMS *Puncher* during the Second World War, and two earlier light fleet carriers, HMCS *Warrior* and "the Maggie", HMCS *Magnificent*.

At this point in her career, *Bonaventure* carried twin-engined Tracker aircraft for use principally in anti-submarine warfare. They carried sonobuoys which would be dropped in the vicinity of a submarine contact to try to locate it using sonar, and homing torpedoes which, when dropped close enough to the target submarine, would search for and hopefully destroy it.

A vital and dangerous function of a destroyer escorting a carrier was that of plane guard. The destroyer would steam close enough to the carrier to be able to rescue the crew of an aircraft that fell into the sea from an unsuccessful catapult launch or landing. Any misunderstanding between the carrier and the plane guard destroyer could very quickly lead to a collision, and the destroyer would not come off best. The Australian *Daring* class destroyer HMAS *Voyager* was cut in two by the aircraft carrier HMAS *Melbourne* in this way on the night of February 10, 1964, with 81 officers and men and one dockyard employee being lost. The second *Athabaskan* is reputed to have had a narrow escape from a similar fate.

Bonaventure Fuelling Chaudière

The *Restigouche* class destroyer escort HMCS *Chaudière* is seen fuelling from *Bonaventure*, this shot having been taken perhaps half an hour prior to the previous photo. For *Chaudière*, the Bonnie was little more than a floating gas station at this point, though a very welcome one indeed after having spent several days at sea on exercises.

Fuelling at sea is an interesting evolution. The tanker, or in this case the carrier, is designated as guide of the formation, being much less manoeuverable than the smaller ship she is fuelling, and she maintains a steady course and speed. The ship being fuelled then keeps station on the guide, altering her engine revolutions up and down and her course by a degree or two back and forth, to try to stay abeam of the guide at a constant distance away from her. The interaction of the two ships' wakes can build up some pretty impressive seas between them. Curiously, it is often possible for the station-keeping ship to find exactly the right engine revolutions (104 revolutions per minute gave *Chaudière* 15 knots), and for as much as ten minutes at a stretch it will be as if the two ships are in lock-step together, no change in engine revolutions being necessary.

Occasionally this exercise is accompanied by some very black humour. If the tanker starts pumping fuel across before the receiving ship is ready, with the fuelling connection made and valving properly set up, or if the fuelling hose parts or the hose connection at the receiving ship comes undone prematurely, the receiving ship can end up with her upper deck and side blackened with fuel oil. Not a pretty sight!

The tanker or carrier maintains a fairly constant tension on the high wire which supports the fuelling hose. In this way, small variations in the distance between the two ships are accommodated without dragging the hose in the water or stretching it to breaking point.

HMCS Ontario

The light cruiser HMCS *Ontario* is seen with her hands fallen in on the upper deck, either for leaving or entering harbour. Several signal flag hoists are visible, including her call-sign, which is flying from the lower yard on her port side. Her starboard anchor is ready for letting go.

Ontario began her life as HMS *Minotaur*. She was laid down at the yard of Harland & Wolff Ltd. in Belfast on November 20, 1941, launched on July 29, 1943, commissioned as *Ontario* on April 16, 1945, and completed on May 25, 1945. Both *Ontario* and *Quebec* were received as gifts from the United Kingdom Government. She was a sistership of the Royal Navy's cruisers *Swiftsure* and *Superb*.

Her two forward triple 6-inch gun turrets are clearly seen in the photograph, as is their director tower above and abaft the bridge. Her two forward twin 4-inch turrets, on either side of the after funnel, are also visible. These had been removed by the time the second picture was taken. Her torpedo tubes, which were just abaft the after funnel on either side, appear to have been removed.

Photo courtesy DND

Displacement:	8,700 tons (11,480 tons full load)
Dimensions:	Length: 555 ½ ft (o.a). Beam: 63 ft.
Draught:	16½ (mean), 21½ (max.) ft.
Guns:	9-6 inch, 10-4 inch, 20-40 mm. AA. (Quadruple)
Tubes:	6-21 inch
Armour:	4½ inch - 3 inch side
Machinery:	Parsons geared turbines. 4 shafts. S.H.P.: 72,500 = 31.5 kts
Boilers:	4 Admiralty 3-drum type
Oil fuel	1,850 tons
Complement	730

Photo courtesy DND

HMCS Ontario

HMCS *Ontario* is getting under way in HMC Dockyard, Esquimalt, with an awning rigged on her quarterdeck. The fo'c'sle party is fallen in, but not in as sharp a fashion as in the preceding photograph. This view from a little more abeam shows her crane, and her four Carley floats secured just abaft her bridge. Her after director tower is visible just abaft her main mast.

Jane's Fighting Ships' statement of her particulars is given here, as cruisers have not been seen in the Canadian Navy for 40 years.

Her 6-inch guns, incidentally, fired a 112-pound shell, using a 30-pound cordite charge, and could achieve a maximum range of 24,800 yards. A rate of fire of 8 rounds per minute per gun was possible. All except one of her 4-inch gun turrets had been removed by the time this picture was taken.

HMCS Quebec

The light cruiser HMCS *Quebec* is doing full-power trials off Esquimalt after re-commissioning in January 1952. Capt. P.D. Budge, RCN, was her commanding officer at that time. He is said to be the only man who began as a boy seaman to reach the rank of Rear Admiral. He is also reported to have taken a Hammond organ to sea with him in *Quebec*, only to have it come adrift in a storm with disastrous results! He died in 1998 at the age of 93. *Quebec* was an ex-*Colony* class RN cruiser, originally being HMS *Uganda*. At the time this photograph was taken, she was doing 32.5 knots.

Uganda was laid down at Vickers-Armstrong Ltd. on the Tyne, on July 20, 1939, launched on August 7, 1941, and completed on January 3, 1943. She was presented to the Royal Canadian Navy by Great Britain on October 21, 1944. Her RN sister ships included HMS *Ceylon*, HMS *Gambia*, HMS *Kenya* and HMS *Newfoundland*. As *Uganda* she had been undergoing a long refit and modernization in the United States during November 1943, when it was decided to present her to Canada. She had been hit aft by a glider bomb on September 13, 1943 while supporting the Salerno landings. Her name was changed to *Quebec* on January 14, 1952.

Here she is seen with the bridge awning frame rigged. Curiously, she carried many more Carley floats on the sides of her forward superstructure than did *Ontario*.

The only differences between her particulars and those of *Ontario* are as follows:

Displacement:	8,000 tons 10,840 tons full load
Dimensions:	Beam: 62 ft
Guns:	9 6-inch, 8 4-inch, 12 2-pdr, 8 40-mm. AA
Armour:	4 inch - 3 inch side
Machinery:	SHP: 72,000 = 31 kts.

Photo courtesy DND

HMCS Sioux

HMCS *Algonquin* and HMCS *Sioux*, laid down as HMS *Valentine* and HMS *Vixen* respectively, became part of the Canadian Navy in February 1944, having been built for the Royal Navy as intermediate fleet V-class destroyers. *Sioux* is seen in the photograph at right.

These ships were originally armed with four 4.7-inch guns in four single-gun turrets, eight 21-inch torpedo tubes, in quadruple mountings, four 40-mm and four 20-mm guns, and were capable of 36 knots. *Sioux* saw service in the Second World War off Norway, in the D-Day operations, and on the Murmansk run. She also did three tours of duty in the Korean War. Before she was paid off in 1963, she had lost one of her torpedo mountings and her after two 4.7-inch turrets, but had acquired two triple-barreled Squid depth charge mortars.

Photo courtesy DND

HMCS Crusader

HMCS *Crescent* and HMCS *Crusader* were loaned to the Canadian Navy by the Royal Navy in 1945, though after VJ-day, and their transfer to the RCN was made permanent in 1951. They were almost identical to *Algonquin* and *Sioux*, differing principally in having only one quadruple torpedo mounting, and 4.5-inch rather than 4.7-inch guns. *Crusader* is seen in the photograph at left. *Crescent*, like *Algonquin*, was converted to a fast anti-submarine frigate, emerging from her conversion in 1956. *Crusader* carried out two tours of duty in the Korean War.

At this stage in her life, *Crusader* was fitted with prototype Variable Depth Sonar (VDS) on her stern, this having necessitated the removal of her aftermost 4.5-inch gun turret. Her sistership *Crescent* carried on the development of VDS after her conversion.

Photo courtesy DND

HMCS Athabaskan (2nd)

The *Tribal* class destroyer escort HMCS *Athabaskan* is closing *Algonquin* from astern for a light line transfer in the summer of 1964. This is the second Canadian destroyer to bear the name, her predecessor having been sunk in an action in the English Channel on April 29, 1944. The second *Athabaskan* saw action in the Korean War. Her successor, the third ship to bear the name, is a member of the later and very different Canadian *Tribal* class, represented in this book by HMCS *Iroquois*.

By the time this photograph was taken, "Atha-B" was the sole *Tribal* still in commission, all but one of her sisters having been paid off and sold for scrap. Fortunately, *Haida* was preserved at Ontario Place, just west of downtown Toronto.

This photograph clearly shows her two twin 4-inch gun turrets forward, and their director tower above her open bridge. The line from the fo'c'sle along the ship's side is her boat rope, correctly rigged from the fo'c'sle back to her motor cutter, so that when the cutter is lowered, the ship's motion through the water will pull the motor cutter forward, and with its tiller lashed to starboard, the cutter will quickly shear away from the ship. She is flying flag "Romeo" from a starboard signal halyard to indicate she is engaged in a transfer operation, and is coming alongside starboard side-to.

HMCS Athabaskan (2nd)

This view of HMCS *Athabaskan* was taken from *Algonquin* while steaming in line abreast during the summer of 1964. Prior to her conversion in 1954, she had six 4.7-inch guns in three turrets, and two 4-inch guns in a fourth turret, but here she is showing her four 4-inch guns in two turrets forward, and her single 3-inch twin turret aft. Her two triple-barreled Squid anti-submarine mortars which she acquired during her conversion are visible on her quarterdeck, almost at the stern.

She is flying flag "Golf", indicating she is guide of the formation. B turret is plainly trained directly at *Algonquin*, and a fire hose is discharging overboard by her torpedo tubes. Her open bridge is immediately abaft B turret, and above and abaft the bridge is the director for her 4-inch armament.

These ships were much faster than the *St. Laurent* class DDEs which followed them. On a full power trial in early 1966, *Athabaskan* was able to reach 35 knots with only two of her three boilers connected, there being some difficulty with connecting the third one. Now with the advent of the marine gas turbine, Canadian warships are once again capable of showing a real turn of speed.

HMC Dockyard, Halifax

Destroyers are lying in HMC Dockyard, Halifax, in early 1964, seen looking south from the Angus L. Macdonald Bridge. The ships' upper decks, the jetties, and the roofs of buildings are white from a recent snowfall. Both ships in the foreground are *Restigouche* class destroyer escorts, as are the outboard two in the group next astern. The inboard ship is either *St. Laurent*, or *Assiniboine*, both newly converted to helicopter carrying destroyer escorts, readily identifiable by the twin funnels on either side of the helicopter hangar. The furthest group from the camera consists of three *Tribals* and *Crescent* outboard. Georges Island is visible in front of McNabs Island at the top left, and the Citadel is at top right of the photograph, downtown Halifax lying between the two. The Halifax skyline has changed almost beyond recognition since this photograph was taken.

Radar Frequency Bands

Captions of several of the subsequent photographs in this book identify the radars on various warships, together with the frequency bands in which those radars operate. The following tables define those frequency bands, both IEEE (Institute of Electrical and Electronics Engineers), and ECM (Electronic Countermeasures) frequency bands.

IEEE Bands

Band	Frequency GHz	Wavelength cm
L	1 to 2	30.00 to 15.00
S	2 to 4	15.00 to 7.50
C	4 to 8	7.50 to 3.75
X	8 to 12	3.75 to 2.50
Ku	12 to 18	2.50 to 1.67
K	18 to 27	1.67 to 1.11
Ka	27 to 40	1.11 to 0.75
mm	40 to 300	0.75 to 0.10

Notes
1 Giga Hertz = 1,000,000,000 cycles per second
Frequency (cycles/second) x Wavelength (cm) = 30,000,000,000 cm/sec, the speed of light.

ECM Bands

Band	Frequency GHz	Wavelength cm
A	0.1 to 0.25	300.00 to 120.00
B	0.25 to 0.5	120.00 to 60.00
C	0.5 to 1	60.00 to 30.00
D	1 to 2	30.00 to 15.00
E	2 to 3	15.00 to 10.00
F	3 to 4	10.00 to 7.50
G	4 to 6	7.50 to 5.00
H	6 to 8	5.00 to 3.75
I	8 to 10	3.75 to 3.00
J	10 to 20	3.00 to 1.50
K	20 to 40	1.50 to 0.75
L	40 to 60	0.75 to 0.50
M	60 to 100	0.50 to 0.30

HMCS Algonquin (1st)

HMCS *Algonquin* is alongside the Imperoyal fuelling jetty in Halifax harbour in 1964. It was very handy to be able to pull up to Imperial Oil's Dartmouth Refinery jetty, and say "Fill 'er up!" Not so handy was the single phone on the jetty from which to make personal calls while the ship was fuelling!

Algonquin began life as a Royal Navy "V" class destroyer, HMS *Valentine*, as did her sister ship *Sioux*, formerly HMS *Vixen*. A major refit by HMC Dockyard, Esquimalt, in 1954 converted *Algonquin* to a fast anti-submarine frigate, and gave her a fully enclosed bridge and two anti-submarine triple-barreled depth bomb Limbo mountings, completely altering her silhouette. She was given an American 3-inch 50-calibre twin gun mounting on her fo'c'sle, and this was later enclosed in a fibreglass weather shield. *Sioux* did not receive this conversion, but kept her original configuration throughout her life. Calibre in this context means that the length of the gun barrel is 50 times the barrel's bore diameter.

In this view her starboard anchor is "a-cockbill", ready for letting go. The round radar antenna for the forward 3-inch-50 gun mounting's fire-control system is visible, mounted atop the gun shield. The three radar antennas visible on the mast are, from the top down, the AN/SPS-10B, the AN/SPS-6C, and the Sperry Marine Radar - MK 2.

HMCS Algonquin (1st) and Argus Aircraft

An Argus aircraft flying over the foremast of *Algonquin* illustrates the co-operation between the RCN and the RCAF in anti-submarine warfare. In spite of the impression given by the photograph, the Argus was not "fly-by-wire", at least not in the modern sense!

The Canadair CL-28 Argus incorporated the wings, tail surfaces, flight controls and undercarriage of the Bristol Britannia, and became a very capable shore-based anti-submarine aircraft. The Britannia was a turbo-prop aircraft, but the Argus had Wright radial air-cooled engines. Its long distinctive tail "stinger" incorporated the so-called "MAD" gear, its magnetic anomaly detector for submarine detection. It was able to drop sonobuoys and homing torpedoes. Some of its anti-submarine search patterns required it to fly very low over the sea, with little margin for error. In the spring of 1965 an Argus dipped a wing in the sea at night north of Puerto Rico, and there were no survivors.

Sonobuoys contain a miniature sonar set, and can be dropped from aircraft. They are then capable of radioing their signals back to the aircraft. One submarine search technique was to drop a pattern of sonobuoys in the area likely to contain a submarine, and then "bomb" the buoys with explosive charges. The echoes of the explosions bouncing off the submarine, together with explosions themselves would be detected by the sonobuoys. From the time delays in arrival of the various buoys' signals the submarine's position could be deduced.

The diamond-shaped wire structure at the top of *Algonquin's* mast is a radio direction-finding device. The curved metal band directly below the aircraft is the AN/SPS-10B radar antenna, and the much larger curved structure midway up the right-hand edge of the photograph, is the AN/SPS-6C radar antenna, with its two distinctive wind balancing vanes. It is facing to port, though when in use, both these antennas constantly rotate to search all around the horizon for either ships or aircraft. The ship's Sperry Marine Mk 2 navigational radar is invisible, forward of and below the larger antenna.

HMCS Algonquin (1st) Limbo Armament

The starboard Limbo mounting is visible in this picture of HMCS *Algonquin* looking forward from her quarterdeck. The port Limbo mounting is in a well slightly further forward. The Limbo is an ahead-throwing depth charge mortar, and is an improvement over the earlier Squid mortar which had three barrels fixed in a yoke which could only be tilted to port and starboard about a fore and aft horizontal centreline. The Limbo's three barrels can be tilted up and down together within their tilting yoke, allowing a much greater variation in target range and bearing. The Limbo's barrels are arranged so that the bombs ideally form a pattern around the target submarine, three bombs exploding above and three below. In reality, temperature layering of the sea refracts a sonar beam, and an experienced submarine skipper will take advantage of this in his attempts to escape an attacking destroyer. Even when the destroyer has measured the sea temperature versus depth profile, using her bathythermograph, it is still quite difficult for her to determine the submarine's location precisely. The winch for lowering the "bathy" over the side is visible to the right of the Limbo mounting. The inboard end of the boom from which it is lowered is at the extreme right edge of the photo.

The main advantage of the Limbo, Squid, and hedgehog over the earlier depth charges was that they could throw their depth bombs ahead of the ship towards a submerged submarine target, before the submarine's sonar echo was lost in the turbulent water underneath the attacking ship. The Limbo and Squid mortars would be trained on the target as determined by sonar, and depth settings electrically fed to the bombs before firing.

Also visible in this photograph, on the upper deck forward of the Limbo is the 4-inch gun turret, trained to port. These guns are Second World War vintage and are hand-loaded, in contrast to today's fully automatic designs. The gun's crew had virtually no protection from incoming enemy fire. However, in peace-time, the brass shell casings did make very nice ashtrays!

HMCS Algonquin (1st)

This is the port side of HMCS *Algonquin*, looking aft from the flag deck at the back of her pilotage position above her forward superstructure. Her port 40-mm single Bofors and her motor cutter davits are visible, as is the White Ensign, flying from a gaff at her mainmast, its usual position at sea. Two of her whip antennas are also visible. Her port flag locker is at the left edge of the picture, the Kisbie ring, or life-buoy, being just in front of it. The large curved black surface at the left edge of the photograph is the back of one of her 20-inch signal lamps. The sky was almost cloudless, and the sea beautifully calm on this particular day in the summer of 1964, as her wake clearly shows her last course alteration, perhaps a mile or so astern of her present position.

This view barely shows the location of the port Limbo mounting. Just above the top of the after davit, directly above the boat falls, one can see a short stack, one of the diesel generator exhausts, and immediately to its left can be seen the nearest barrel of the port Limbo projecting above the upper deck from its well.

HMCS Crescent

HMCS *Crescent* is abeam of *Algonquin* in the summer of 1964 after her conversion to a destroyer escort, or DDE. *Algonquin* and *Crescent* were very similar in appearance, both having twin 3-inch 50-calibre and twin 4-inch mountings. *Algonquin* had her 3-inch 50 mounting forward and her twin 4-inch turret aft. *Crescent* had just the opposite arrangement.

The structure at *Crescent's* stern is a retractable frame and winch to lower her variable depth sonar (VDS) transducer over her stern. Lowering the sonar transducer below some, hopefully all, of the refracting temperature layers, will reduce the distortion of the submarine's true position, greatly increasing the chances of a kill. Her port Limbo's three barrels are visible just abaft the 3-inch-50 turret.

Algonquin, with an almost identical silhouette to *Crescent*, had a large open pilotage position above her bridge from where the ship could be conveniently conned. In fine warm weather it was particularly good not to be in the enclosed bridge and have a much better view all around the ship, from a somewhat higher vantage point. The open pilotage position was continued in the *St. Laurent* class, but the *Restigouche* class was not fitted with a gyro compass repeater on the platform above the bridge, and thus could only be conned from the enclosed bridge. Gyro repeaters were fitted in the bridge wings of the *Restigouche* class, however, these being helpful for coming alongside, anchoring, and replenishment at sea.

HMCS Stettler

The frigate HMCS *Stettler*, is following *Sussexvale* southbound through Sansom Narrows, between Vancouver Island and Saltspring Island, during a cadet pilotage training cruise in the early summer of 1960.

Twenty-one frigates were converted to the *Prestonian* design with an enclosed bridge and an upper deck carried all the way aft, giving a higher quarterdeck. However only seven of these ships were given a cadet training classroom, or gunroom, abaft the funnel, with hooded chart tables and gyro compass repeaters for navigation training on the deck above the gunroom. These ships were ideal for cadet training, and in the early sixties the seven with the gunroom were based in Esquimalt and used for Regular Officer Training Plan (ROTP) cadet training during the summers. Those based in Halifax were able to take University Naval Training Divisions (UNTD) cadets for summer training.

The armament of these ships consisted of one twin 4-inch gun turret forward, a single 40-mm Bofors gun each side of the forward superstructure, a twin 40-mm Bofors mounting aft, and two triple-barreled anti-submarine Squid mountings in a well below the quarterdeck. Their machinery consisted of two 4-cylinder triple expansion engines. The two boilers were in separate, closed boiler rooms, entered via airlocks.

Stettler has her port anchor "a-cockbill", ready for letting go, since there is little room for error in this channel, and it is very likely that a second year cadet was navigating her at the time!

A small wooden boat is lying upside down atop the covers over her Squid well on her quarterdeck, just forward of the stern. Being at anchor her boat booms are rigged, visible at her stern, as is her accommodation ladder platform, at right on her port side. Her whaler davits are empty, and the whaler together with the motor cutter appear to be secured at the port boat boom. Normally-travelled walkways on the decks are clearly outlined by the patterns of non-skid pads glued to the decks. Without these, walking along wet decks in any sort of a sea would be much too hazardous.

The view forward from the mast of Sussexvale shows her pilotage position, directly above her enclosed bridge, and her 4-inch gun turret and fo'c'sle. The lookouts' swivel chairs are visible on either side of the chart table hood, with their binocular mounts, from which can be read the bearing and elevation of a contact. The ship was at anchor in Plumper Sound, between Pender and Saturna Islands, in the Gulf Islands between Victoria and Vancouver.

These ships could easily be conned from the open pilotage position, but in inclement weather it was very nice to use the totally enclosed bridge immediately below.

Two Bird's-eye Views of HMCS Sussexvale

Looking aft from the mast of HMCS *Sussexvale* shows the top of her cadet training gunroom, with the hooded chart tables and gyro compass repeaters for navigation training.

HMCS Beacon Hill in Jackstay Transfer with Sussexvale

Capt. H.A. Porter, Commander 4th Escort Squadron, is shown in this photograph crossing between *Sussexvale* and *Beacon Hill* in a jackstay transfer while at sea on passage from Esquimalt to Yokohama, via Adak in the Aleutian Islands. "C-4" and his staff would cross by jackstay to a different ship each day, and cadets would man the jackstay, there being typically 24 cadets in each ship. Weather in the North Pacific, however, did not always permit such an evolution!

The jackstay supporting the traveller is made fast to a bracket in the (equipment) receiving ship. At the command "Haul Taut the Jackstay", men in the supplying ship heave on the jackstay so that the man about to cross is hoisted up as he stands with his foot in the stirrup. The receiving ship's men then pull the traveller and its passenger across. One of the two ships is designated as guide, and the other keeps station on her with the aid of a distance line held between the fo'c'sles of the two ships. While the operation is fairly safe, the passenger is well advised to wear his life jacket. People have got their feet wet from time to time!

The 4-inch gun turret is clearly visible in the background, its mechanism protected from the weather by canvas curtains which can be quickly opened when required. The captain's cabin is directly below the gun. Light bulbs in his deckhead fixtures did not last very long!

Two Close-up Views of Stettler

HMCS *Stettler* makes a light-line transfer with *Jonquière*. Her fo'c'sle and forward superstructure are clearly visible. In such a transfer, no jackstay line is rigged.

These ships had both a fully-enclosed bridge, whose four port-side windows are visible, and an open pilotage position above. From this it was possible to con the ship in good weather, with much better all around visibility. All one lacked on the pilotage position was the radar display. The wheelhouse, incidentally, was at the back of the bridge, and unlike the practice in some ships, the helmsman could only follow the orders of the officer-of-the-watch and steer a compass course, being completely unable to see where the ship was going. Just forward of the bridge one can see the back of the 4-inch gun turret, mounted directly above the CO's cabin. One deck below the enclosed bridge, on its own platform deck, is the port 40-mm single-barreled Bofors gun.

The port 10-inch signal projector is just to the left of the forward whip antenna on the side of the pilotage position, and the 20-inch signal projector is visible above the port flag locker, the array of pigeon holes in the cabinet at the top of the vertical ladder. Officer cadets had their fair share of flag hoisting drills, and woe betide the miserable sinner who hoisted a flag without its down-haul halyard being buttoned on! The Sperry radar's antenna is visible up the tripod mast, and above it the dome of the more primitive SU radar, which was only capable of giving an "A-trace", rather than PPI, or plan position indicator display. The signal flag flying is flag "Romeo", to indicate that a transfer between two ships is in progress.

This photograph of *Stettler* taken during the same transfer as the previous photo, shows the gunroom and training pilotage position above with chart tables and gyro repeaters. Another pair of frigates is in the distance, also making a transfer.

The gunroom for cadets undergoing training served as wardroom, classroom, and dining room. It was situated directly over the engine room, and so was u-shaped to permit the engine room skylight to remain unobstructed. This structure was only fitted in the seven west-coast frigates, *Antigonish, Beacon Hill, Jonquière, New Glasgow, Ste. Thérèse, Stettler,* and *Sussexvale*. Regular Officer Training Plan (ROTP) cadets were fortunate to train in these ships in the early sixties. University Naval Training Division (UNTD) cadets who trained on the east coast were not so lucky, without such a dedicated facility.

The whaler and motor cutter's after ends are visible at left, as they hang in the davits. Two of the four hooded chart tables are visible behind the two cadets on top of the gunroom. Just forward of the cadets is one of two gyro compass repeaters, all of these facilities being specially fitted for cadet training. It was here that cadets would take and plot navigational sights, fixing the ship's position during in-shore pilotage training, or taking sun or star sights for astro navigation. The canvas-wrapped structure at extreme right, at the after end of the deck above the gunroom, is the director for the 40-mm twin Bofors gun mounting, the gun itself being on the quarter deck, just abaft this deck house.

Canadian Warships

Photo courtesy DND

HMCS St. Laurent as Originally Built

The destroyer escort (DDE) HMCS *St. Laurent*, possibly in the St. Lawrence River near Montreal, is shown as originally built, before being commissioned. The *St. Laurent* class DDE was the first class of warship completely designed and built in Canada. With their rounded bow, their anchors in pockets, and their mast with its enclosed base, they were quite a novel design. Due to their hull design's giving them a very high righting moment, they were somewhat uncomfortable in rough weather. However, this made for a very stable weapons platform, in contrast to ships having a long, slow roll. Coming after the *Tribals*, they were quickly dubbed "the Cadillacs."

The *St. Laurent* and the other six ships of her class were all converted to helicopter carrying destroyer escorts (DDHs) in the mid-sixties, and were given a helicopter hangar, flight deck, and twin funnels. In the process they lost their after 3-inch 50-calibre mounting and one Limbo mounting, but acquired variable depth sonar mounted in the stern. *St. Laurent* is seen after her conversion in the following photograph.

At this very early point in her life, she has not yet acquired fibreglass gun shields which later enclosed her 3-inch-50 Mk 33 FMC gun mountings. Her Limbo well's white painted port bulkhead shows up quite clearly in the photograph, between her ensign staff and her after 3-inch 50 mounting, below the quarterdeck. Two Limbos were fitted here, and were protected from the weather by removable covers when not required. Helicopters could, and did, occasionally land on the Limbo covers, though this was only possible in fairly calm seas, as no helicopter haul-down facilities were fitted.

St. Laurent as a DDH

HMCS *St. Laurent*, now a helicopter-carrying DDH, is berthed alongside HMCS *Gatineau* in Brooklyn Navy Yard in the spring of 1965. This photograph clearly shows the difference between the bridges of the *St. Laurent* and *Restigouche* class, the latter, as typified by *Gatineau*, having a higher bridge structure to give a clear view ahead over the top of the 3-inch-70 gun turret. The *St. Laurent* class, in contrast, was fitted with the 3-inch-50 twin gun mounting forward. As this did not have the complex shell handling mechanism the 3-inch-70 required, it could be mounted lower down on the fo'c'sle, resulting in a lower bridge structure than on the *Restigouche* class.

The conversion of these ships to DDHs necessitated their boiler uptakes being split into a pair of funnels, one on either side of the helicopter hangar. The funnels of *St. Laurent* and *Assiniboine* were given nicely faired, sloping tops, whereas the other seven DDHs all had less attractive flat-topped funnels. Though not visible here, the *St. Laurent* class received the VDS in their conversion, this necessitating a modification to the stern. On the negative side, the conversion to DDH of these ships sacrificed the 3-inch-50 gun mounting on the quarterdeck, as well as one of the two Limbo mountings, the latter resulting in a salvo consisting of only three, rather than six mortar bombs. However, gaining a sea-going Sea King helicopter, complete with dunking sonar and homing torpedoes, certainly outweighed these sacrifices.

Another nice comparison is between the open port anchor pocket door on *St. Laurent* and the closed anchor pocket door on *Gatineau*. These doors were normally kept closed when the anchors were fully home, either in harbour or at sea. Another contrast is between the newer upper lattice foremast in *St. Laurent*, and the earlier solid upper foremast in *Gatineau*.

HMCS Gatineau as Originally Built

The *Restigouche* class destroyer escort HMCS *Gatineau* is seen abeam of *Chaudière* at the mouth of the Delaware River on November 22, 1963, the day President Kennedy was shot. The seven-ship *Restigouche* class followed on from the *St. Laurent* class, but with two distinctive features. The forward 3-inch 50-calibre American mounting was replaced by a 3-inch 70-calibre Vickers twin turret. Bridge wings were added, which gave excellent visibility for bringing the ship alongside a jetty, or handling her during replenishment-at-sea evolutions.

Gatineau is seen wearing a thin black stripe around her funnel, indicating she is the second-most senior ship in the squadron. *Chaudière*, carrying the squadron commander and his staff, wore a broad black band around her funnel.

The Restigouche Class Bow

The *Restigouche* class DDE HMCS *Chaudière* is being brought up on the Dartmouth Slips, in December 1963. The chains which pull up the table on which she is being lifted are clearly visible. This highlights her uniquely Canadian rounded bow, with its anchor pockets closed by hinged doors. With this bow design these ships were much more inclined to ride over a sea, rather than burrow through it.

HMC Dockyard, Halifax, did not have its own dry-docking facilities, but was dependent upon Halifax Shipyards' drydock and floating dock, or the Dartmouth Slips. To come up on the slips, a ship would be carefully lined up and secured over the centreline of the table, and then stacks of blocks would be winched inwards to contact her hull before the table was pulled up the inclined railway to haul her out of the water.

Gatineau has just hit a green one in this photograph, at right, taken from the starboard bridge wing, while proceeding to assist the burning trawler *Karen B* off Eastern Nova Scotia in early 1966. *Gatineau* was steaming at at least 26 knots. As usual when at sea, her jackstaff has been stowed, and only the tripod which supports it remains in place. Her breakwater is visible just forward of the 3-inch-70 turret, which is trained aft to give it some protection from the seas. Standing on the bridge of a warship looking practically down her gun barrels always felt just a bit strange, in spite of knowing that electrical interlocks would not allow the guns to fire into her own superstructure.

On HMCS Chaudière's Bridge

"Sir, there are trees ahead!" Inside the bridge of *Chaudière*, while transiting the Kiel Canal in the summer of 1963, Captain C.P. Nixon, Commander, 5th Escort Squadron, is briefed by Lieutenant-Commander W.G. Welbourn, a member of his staff. Commander R.H. Falls, *Chaudière's* CO, sits in his chair at the left. Sub-Lieutenant Walt Henry, officer-of-the-watch, is conning the ship, standing at the pelorus, the main gyro compass repeater. Commander Falls, affectionately referred to as "Father", went on to become Chief of the Defence Staff in 1977. Was Naval Headquarters thinking of Chaudière Falls, near Quebec City, when it appointed him CO of *Chaudière*?

Having the squadron commander and his staff riding in one's ship could lead to a crowded bridge and operations room, even though all these ships were fitted out as destroyer leaders. The captain would have to share his cabin with the squadron commander, and having six or eight squadron staff on board could occasionally lead to frayed tempers. A wise executive officer would invite his captain down to the wardroom each evening at sea to give him a break from his boss.

Restigouche Class's Original Mast

This is HMCS *Chaudière's* mast showing her ship's badge and her Sperry, AN/SPS 10 and AN/SPS 12 radar antennas. The 5th Escort Squadron Commander's pennant flies at the mast head, indicating he is riding in *Chaudière* with his staff. The Sperry, a high definition warning surface radar, is the lowest of the three radar antennas, and was used principally for navigation and collision avoidance. The upper two radars are longer range surface and air warning sets, the larger AN/SPS 12, and the upper and smaller AN/SPS 10. These radar antennas rotated at 15 rpm. "MUF DUF" and "HUF DUF", medium and high frequency radio direction finding antennas, together with aircraft warning lights, are other items "up the stick". Unfortunately a black and white photograph fails to do justice to her barber pole stripes.

This mast design was not without its problems. The executive officer of *Fraser*, LCdr John Norman, had the unpleasant duty one night of reporting to his commanding officer, Cdr D.L. MacKnight, that the upper part of the mast had come down. The latter's reaction was not recorded! The upper part of the mast of the *Mackenzie* class DDEs, which followed the *Restigouche* class, was modified to a lattice design, likely as a result of the failure in *Fraser*. The entire masts of the four *Restigouche* class ships which were given the DELEX (destroyer life extension) refit, as well as those of *Annapolis* and *Nipigon*, were later replaced by a higher, entirely lattice design.

Modern Marine Radars
AN/SPS-10B (Modified)

The AN/SPS-10B (modified) was a medium range, C-band, good definition, surface warning set with a limited air capability. In the Canadian Forces, this type was only used in shipborne installations and training facilities. It was used for the detection, ranging and tracking of surface contacts and to a limited extent, air contacts as well. Range and bearing information was passed to a PPI type display. This radar type had the potential to be used with IFF/SIF equipment so the SPS-10 was originally fitted with a built in beacon. The RCN never used this feature, so it was disabled. There never was a model SPS-10A.

AN/SPS-12

Radar set AN/SPS-12 was an L-band, medium surveillance radar designed to detect aircraft and surface vessels. It was primarily an air search set and was fitted on the original Canadian DDE class destroyers. In some circles, it was described as an SPS-6 with much greater capability. Target range was presented on an A-type indicator. Bearing data was also provided for presentation on PPI units. Provision was also made to connect IFF (Identification-Friend or Foe) equipment to the radar set.

SPERRY MARINE RADAR - MK 2

This was a medium range, surface search radar designated as a High Definition Warning Surface (HDWS) set. From the early 1950's, until well into the 1970's, almost every ship in the RCN was fitted with the Sperry Mk 2. Although its primary use was to locate other ships, helicopters, navigation aids and shorelines, it was very effective in detecting submarine periscopes.

Excerpted from the HMCS Haida web site. This excellent source of information can be found at http://webhome.idirect.com/~jproc/sari/sarrad2.html.

HMCS Terra Nova

The *Restigouche* class DDE HMCS *Terra Nova* tries to emulate a submarine in the act of crash diving, bow digging in and stern far out of the water, as seen from *Provider*. This clearly shows her stern, modified from its original as-built form to accommodate VDS, variable depth sonar. In its original form her stern sloped forward from the waterline up to the upper deck. Now it slopes aft to the upper deck. Her new, much higher, lattice mast shows up clearly in this view. Only four of the seven *Restigouche* class DDEs, *Gatineau*, *Restigouche*, *Kootenay*, and *Terra Nova*, received their DELEX refits, which gave them these modifications.

Photo courtesy VAdm J.A. Fulton (retd)

The Hydrofoil HMCS Bras d'Or

The hydrofoil HMCS *Bras d'Or* is seen at speed, foil-borne, in this photograph. Sadly, this unique 180-ton, 150.8-foot-long vessel's potential was not exploited, and after some very successful trials and demonstration cruises she was de-commissioned.

Bras d'Or was powered by a 30,000 SHP intermittent, 25,500 SHP max continuous Pratt-Whitney FT4-A2 gas turbine when foil-borne, and by a 2,000 BHP Paxman Ventura 16YJCM V-form 16 cylinder, turbocharged four-stroke diesel engine when hull-borne. Her hollow foils were made of extremely high strength (250,000 psi yield strength) 18% NiCoMo maraging steel to withstand the high stresses experienced at full speed. Steering was effected by a hydraulic ram's turning the forward foil structure at the bow. The main foils were fixed, and one of the screws for hull-borne, or displacement mode, operation is visible through the spray in the main foil struts. Her gas turbine main engine was mounted immediately abaft the pilot house in an enclosure on the weather deck, and its exhaust outlet can be seen facing upwards.

During her very short life of just under four years, exhaustive tests were performed of her capabilities, and on one occasion she exceeded her designed 60 knots by 2 knots. See *The Flying 400 - Canada's Hydrofoil Project* by Thomas G. Lynch for an excellent treatment of this unusual vessel.

Photo courtesy Defence Research Establishment Atlantic

Improved Restigouche Class in Harbour

HMCS *Gatineau* and another *Restigouche* class DDE are seen with tall lattice masts, alongside "A" Jetty in HMC Dockyard, Esquimalt, dressed overall, on July 1, 1983. *Gatineau* was outboard, if memory serves. Both ships have undergone refits in which they acquired both ASROC, an anti-submarine rocket replacing the 3-inch 50-calibre gun mounting on the quarterdeck, and variable depth sonar mounted in the stern. These acquisitions necessitated both the removal of one Limbo A/S Mk 10 triple mortar, and changing the stern's profile from sloping forward to sloping aft, gaining five feet of length in the process. At time of writing, August 1998, *Gatineau* is no longer in commission, but is in an extended readiness state, being 39 years old, a very great age for a warship.

The rounded bows of these *Restigouche* class DDEs show quite clearly in this photograph, as does the port bridge wing of the inboard ship. The port navigation light is housed in the recess under this bridge wing. The 3-inch 70-calibre Vickers gun turret of each ship is visible on her fo'c'sle. Both ships are flying the third substitute pennant from their port yards, indicating their captains are ashore. The inboard ship is flying the SCOPA pennant at her starboard yard to indicate she carries the Senior Canadian Officer Present Afloat. The two wheel-shaped objects on pedestals on either side of the mast of the inboard ship are UHF satellite communication antennas. While they are frequently seen both pointing in the same direction, they can be independently trained on different satellites.

Some of the electronic equipment supported by the new lattice mast includes the Tacan URN 25 fitted on a pole mast replacing the top section of the lattice mast. Below that is the small rotating aerial of the surface search Raytheon SPS 10, G band radar. Below the SPS 10 aerial is the larger rotating aerial of what appears to be an SPS 12, L band radar. Finally, immediately above the bridge, between the satellite communications antennas of the inboard ship, can be seen the fire control Bell SPG 48, I/J band radar, mounted atop the director tower. The ship's bow in the foreground is that of USS *O'Callahan*, a *Garcia* class American escort ship (DE).

HMCS Provider Fuelling USS Ticonderoga

This photograph shows HMCS *Provider* fuelling USS *Ticonderoga* (CVS-14). *Ticonderoga* was commissioned in September 1945 as an *Essex* class carrier, but was extensively modernized during the 1950s, being given an enclosed hurricane bow, an angled flight deck, improved elevators, increased aviation fuel storage, and steam catapults. With a displacement of approximately 42,000 tons full load, a length of 894.5 feet, a beam of 103 feet, and a flight deck width of 192 feet, she was able to carry 70 to 80 aircraft. She had eight 600 psi Babcock & Wilcox boilers providing steam to four geared turbines driving four shafts, developing 150,000 shp to give her a speed of over 30 knots. She had a complement of 115 officers, 1,500 enlisted men, and approximately 800 assigned to her ASW airgroup, for a total of just over 2,400. She was decommissioned in 1973.

For comparison purposes, the corresponding particulars of *Bonaventure* are displacement 20,000 tons full load, length 704 feet overall, beam 80 feet, and overall width including angled deck and mirrors 128 feet. *Bonaventure* could carry 34 Banshee and Tracker aircraft. She had four Admiralty 3-drum type 350 psi boilers supplying steam to Parsons single reduction geared turbines driving two shafts, developing 42,000 shp to give her a designed speed of 24.5 knots. In reality, she was known as the only ship in the Navy to have her speed tattooed on her side, namely 22, her pennant number! Her war complement was 1,370.

Provider was the first of three replenishment ships, being followed by *Preserver* and *Protecteur*. She had a light displacement of 7,300 tons, and 22,700 full load, an overall length of 555 feet, a beam of 76 feet, and she could accommodate at least three CH-124A Sea King ASW helicopters in her hangar immediately below the funnel. Her two Combustion Engineering water tube boilers and Westinghouse double reduction geared turbine developing 21,000 shp through one shaft gave her a speed of 20 knots. She had a complement of 11 officers and 131 ratings. Her cargo capacity was 17,340 tons of fuel oil, 665 tons of aviation fuel, and 250 tons of dry cargo. A total of 20 electrohydraulic winches were fitted on deck for ship-to-ship and shore-to-ship movement of cargo and supplies. In an exercise in the Pacific, *Provider* was able to keep three USN Sea King helicopters aloft continuously for a 72-hour period, bringing them down only to refuel and change crews, something of a record.

Photo courtesy USN via VAdm. J.A. Fulton

HMCS Provider Fuelling Algonquin

HMCS *Provider* is seen replenishing HMCS *Algonquin* at sea, in the fall of 1964, when *Provider* was on trials.

Provider was the first of three fleet replenishment vessels built, and was fitted with special hydraulically operated winches to control her fuelling hoses. Her "jungle deck", the lowest open deck visible in the picture, provides access to the piping and valving connecting her tanks to the fuelling pumps and hoses. It was quickly found to be particularly wet in even moderate seas.

Provider has rigged pudding fenders just in case *Algonquin* comes a shade too close! The two hoses suspended from the high wire between the two ships are transferring diesel oil in the smaller hose, and furnace fuel oil in the larger. *Algonquin* required diesel oil for her auxiliary diesel generators. Visible just to the left of the after starboard goalpost mast is a vertical column with a pulley block at its top. This column is driven up and down by a hydraulic ram to tension the cables supporting the fuelling hoses. While an evolution such as refuelling at sea always brings out a goodly number of "goofers", the fact that *Provider* was actually undergoing trials at the time this picture was taken does justify the presence of an extraordinary number of spectators!

Algonquin's men on the upper deck are wearing inflatable life jackets against the possibility of being washed overboard by a heavy sea. The barrels of her port limbo mounting, a triple-barreled depth charge mortar, are seen pointing inboard at approximately 45 degrees. Their covers are in place to avoid ingress of seawater. The radar dish antenna visible at the right hand end of the fuelling hoses is the fire control radar for the 4-inch gun turret just below to the right. This radar, together with the after fire control system in the ship, enables the gun to track and shell a moving target. Projecting above the radar dish are two of the ship's radio whip antennas. While a warship tries to do a great deal more listening than talking to avoid giving away her position to an enemy, communications with friendly forces are vitally important. Just above and to the right of the radar dish the two "Not under Command" spheres are suspended, to show any passing vessel that *Algonquin* cannot easily alter course to get out of the way. *Provider* is showing the same indication just visible at the right hand edge of her after starboard goalpost mast. While emergency breakaway of the ship being fuelled from the tanker is certainly possible, it is far from desirable, and much preferable to advertize to passing vessels that the pair of ships so involved would like to continue on their present course and speed without interruption. It is possible for two ships engaged in replenishment at sea to alter course, but it is difficult, and must be done very carefully and slowly, a few degrees at a time.

HMCS Saskatchewan

The *Mackenzie* class DDE HMCS *Saskatchewan* is seen here in the Inside Passage off the West Coast in the summer of 1993, preparing to take her sistership *Yukon* in tow, as an exercise. Apart from a slightly different mast design, there was virtually no difference between *Mackenzie*, *Saskatchewan*, and *Yukon*, and the original *Restigouche* class.

The stern design common to all four classes, *St. Laurent*, *Restigouche*, *Mackenzie*, and *Annapolis*, is rather curious in that here one gets the false impression that it slopes upward and aft from the waterline. In reality it slopes upward and forward from the waterline, as seen to some extent in the earlier photo of *St. Laurent* in the St. Lawrence River before her commissioning. Only the four *Restigouche* class DDEs which were given a DELEX refit received sterns which sloped upward and aft from the waterline, this to make provision for the variable depth sonar. The 3-inch-70's director tower, with its radar, is seen above the bridge, immediately forward of the foremast.

Like the original *Restigouche* class, the four *Mackenzie* class ships, apart from *Qu'appelle* which had 3-inch 50-calibre mountings forward and aft, had one 3-inch 70-calibre twin turret forward, one 3-inch-50 calibre twin mounting aft, two triple barreled Limbo mountings in a well below the quarterdeck, and homing torpedoes thrown from launchers in the after superstructure.

Photo courtesy SLt. Geoffrey Steed

Photo courtesy SLt. Geoffrey Steed

HMCS Annapolis Berthed on Provider

HMCS *Annapolis* is berthed alongside the supply ship HMCS *Provider*, in HMC Dockyard, Esquimalt, in the summer of 1993. She was the second of two DDHs (helicopter carrying destroyer escorts) originally built as such.

This photograph shows her with her lattice mast, which she received in her DELEX major refit in 1985-86. At time of writing, August 1998, *Provider* is awaiting disposal, having just paid off. Most of the *St. Laurent*, *Restigouche*, *Mackenzie*, and *Annapolis* class destroyer escorts have been broken up or sunk to create artificial reefs. None remain in commission.

Provider has her starboard anchor down, which she may have used in coming alongside the jetty, and also she is displaying her fuelling hoses at her forward goalpost masts. It is possible that *Provider* was actually fuelling *Annapolis* at the time the picture was taken, though jetty space may have been scarce, necessitating *Annapolis* berthing on *Provider*. The starboard anchor pocket door of *Annapolis* is closed, and the similarity between her and the *St. Laurent* class conversions to helicopter carrying destroyers is easily seen. Like those ships, she carried an American 3-inch 50-calibre twin mounting on her fo'c'sle. Her breakwater protecting it can just be made out.

Squid and Limbo

These four photographs show both a frigate's and a DDE's quarterdeck, with the Squid and Limbo mortar well covers, and the Squid and Limbo mountings themselves. At left is *Sussexvale*, and at right is one of her Squid mountings.

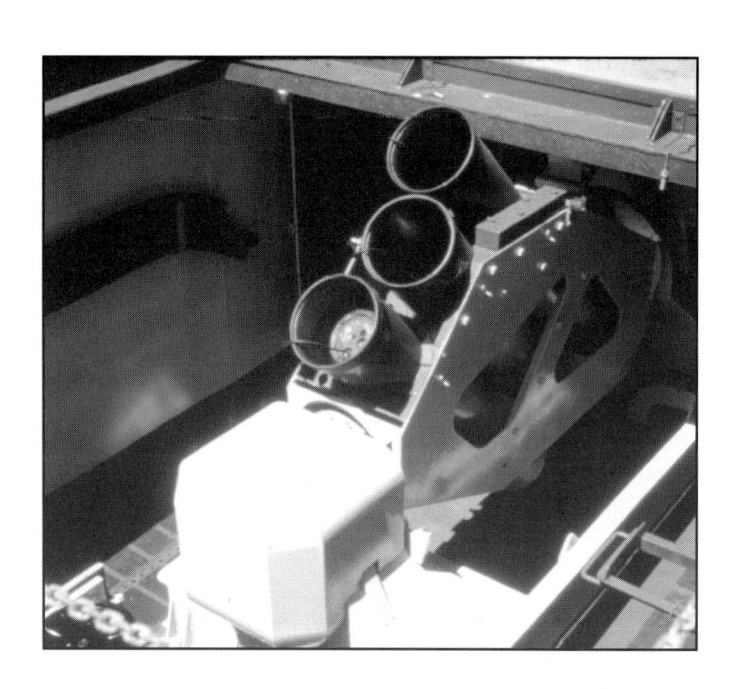

In the photo at left, *Bonaventure's* HU-21 HO4S-3 helicopter "Pedro" is being talked down onto *Chaudière's* Limbo well covers by her executive officer, LCdr J.W. "Deac" Logan, a former "fly boy" himself, and bottom right, *Annapolis'* single Limbo mounting.

HMCS Terra Nova in Later Life

This 1995 view of HMCS *Terra Nova* very clearly shows the distinctive features of the four improved *Restigouche* class DDEs, *Gatineau*, *Kootenay*, *Restigouche*, and *Terra Nova*, which underwent the conversion which gave them the tall lattice mast, ASROC and VDS. The only change from the original design of these ships forward of the bridge is the loss of the anchor pocket door, whose mechanism gave trouble in later life. However, immediately abaft the bridge the changes become quite significant. A tall lattice mast with quite different radar antennas has replaced the original distinctive mast design, and what appears to be a new short tower fitted immediately forward of the mast, but just abaft the 3-inch-70 gun's director tower is actually a structure supporting two satellite communications antennas, one on each side. The funnel is unchanged, but the after "house" has changed considerably, and the short mainmast has disappeared completely. Immediately abaft the after house, the anti-submarine rocket mounting has replaced the 3-inch-50 gun. This is the Honeywell ASROC Mk 112 octuple launcher, the large horizontal box-like structure. Further aft, on the quarterdeck, one of the triple torpedo tube launchers can be made out, and finally, the modified stern to house VDS, the variable depth sonar. *Terra Nova* was fitted with the Phalanx Mk 15 gun just abaft the torpedo tubes when she served in the Persian Gulf in 1991/92.

Photo courtesy DND

HMCS Gatineau and Terra Nova at Extended Readiness

Gatineau and *Terra Nova* photographed at HMC Dockyard, Halifax in 1998, as they lay at extended readiness, *Gatineau* being inboard. They were berthed at the Dockyard's most northerly jetty, just north of the Angus L. MacDonald bridge, this jetty formerly being known as Jetty Five, if memory serves. The fleet diving support ship *Cormorant* lies just astern of them, awaiting disposal.

These views show close-up detail of these *Restigouche* class ships in their last "incarnation". The forward hull, 3-inch-70 gun, funnel, and forward house have changed very little since these ships were originally built, but their foremast is very different, the after house has changed to accommodate a magazine for Asroc, and the stern has been significantly altered to cater to VDS, as mentioned earlier. Nothing appears to have been removed from these ships in preparation for disposal.

Gatineau's Bridge and Mast

This close-up view of *Gatineau's* bridge and mast clearly shows her two wheel-like satellite communications antennas, and a small T-shaped navigational radar antenna between them, just to the right of the fire control Bell SPG 48 radome atop its director tower. Progressing up the mast, the solid radar antenna is her air search Marconi SPS 503, E/F band, and above it is her surface search Raytheon SPS 10, G Band screen/mesh type radar antenna. Above the top of the lattice mast is her CANEWS (Canadian Electronic Warfare System) radar warning antenna array. *Terra Nova's* 3-inch-70 director tower appears above *Gatineau's* 3-inch-70 gun. I have to admit to feeling that the original, as-built, appearance of these ships was a great detail less cluttered, and much more aesthetically pleasing. However, they had become much more capable warships.

Gatineau's Superstructure

Finally, the view from just abeam shows how her after "house" was modified to accommodate the magazine for Asroc, the latter being the large rectangular box-like structure at the right hand edge of the photograph. The house, or more properly, the after superstructure, had previously contained the ASW homing torpedo throwers and magazine, as well as the hull mechanics' shop. Note that the boat davits and small stump mast have disappeared. The curious honeycomb appearance of the hull plating of these ships shows up prominently in this photograph. These ships were the first Canadian warships to be built with an all-welded hull, and it would appear that the post-weld stress relieving left a little to be desired, as one can clearly see the grid of her frames and longitudinal members beneath her hull plating. The three stacks of Nova Scotia Power's Tufts Cove Generating Station, across the harbour, appear just above *Gatineau's* fo'c'sle.

HMCS Assiniboine's Variable Depth Sonar

HMCS *Assiniboine* is alongside Pugsley Pier in Saint John. When first completed in 1956 she was identical to the lead ship of her class, *St. Laurent*, with a completely clean stern. She was the first *St. Laurent* class DDE to complete conversion to DDH. *St. Laurent* and *Assiniboine* were the only two DDHs to have the tops of their twin funnels sloped aft, all the others having less aesthetically pleasing flat tops to their funnels, as on *Annapolis*.

Her variable depth sonar (VDS) is very prominent, mounted at her stern. This development was the first design in Canadian ships to be able to lower a sonar transducer below the sound-refracting temperature layers in the sea, significantly below the more usual keel-fixed sonar dome. In this way, depending upon the sea temperature versus depth profile, a much more reliable sonar indication of a submerged submarine could be obtained, making it more difficult for a submarine to hide.

The VDS drogue is suspended from a special cable passing over the large pulley at the top of the rectangular frame which pivots about bearings secured to the stern, directly above the hull numbers "2" and "4". To deploy the drogue, the frame is pivoted aft about its bearings, so that the drogue is suspended over the water. Its cable is then paid out to lower it into the sea, to the appropriate depth.

A Variable Depth Sonar Drogue

This is the VDS drogue of HMCS *Ottawa*. It houses the sonar transducer, and is deployed over the stern at the end of a special cable. It can be towed at various depths, depending upon the parent ship's speed and the length of cable paid out. VDS has now been superseded by "Cantass", Canadian towed array sonar, in which a special sensor cable is paid out through a round opening in the stern. This development has greatly increased the ability to detect a submarine, and apparently USN nuclear submarine commanders have been amazed at the distances at which they have first been detected by Canadian warships.

Photo courtesy SLt. Geoffrey Steed

Below is a close-up view of the "bear trap" under a Sea King helicopter, which makes helicopter operations possible from the rolling deck of a destroyer at sea. A trolley contains a pair of jaws which, when closed, securely hold a prong which projects down from the helicopter. The helicopter can then be hauled forward into the ship's helicopter hangar. The hollow square frame immediately to the right of the helicopter's landing gear is the bear trap itself, with the track in the ship's flight deck along which it runs, leading to the right. The helicopter may be safely moved into or out of the hangar by winching the bear trap along the track. This shot was taken when the ship was open to visitors, hence the rope to keep people back from the Sea King. The photograph also shows the Sea King's starboard twin-wheel retractable landing gear and stabilizing float.

Sea King Helicopter and Bear Trap

A Sea King helicopter flies by the port quarter of HMCS *Athabaskan* in early 1966. "Atha B" had proceeded to sea off Halifax for a full power trial, and by then was the only surviving *Tribal*. Unfortunately her third boiler could not be connected, but she managed 34 knots on two boilers. She was not wasting any time when this photograph was taken! Two of her 40-mm Bofors are visible pointing outboard at a suitably offensive elevation. This view is looking aft from the bridge, and the top of her after funnel's cap is showing, as well as the after 3-inch 50-calibre gun's weather shield.

The Later Tribals: HMCS Iroquois (2nd)

The later *Tribal* class destroyer escort HMCS *Iroquois* is seen as originally built, in HMC Dockyard, Halifax, in August 1988, sixteen years after she was commissioned. Apart from the purely experimental hydrofoil, *Bras d'Or*, the four ships of this class were the first Canadian warships to be powered by gas turbines.

The *St. Laurent* class DDH *Skeena* is at the adjacent jetty to the left with her stern towards the camera, showing her flight deck, helicopter hangar, and twin funnels.

Iroquois and her three sister ships *Huron*, *Athabaskan* and *Algonquin*, when first commissioned in 1972 and 1973 were armed with a single 5-inch/54 Oto Melara gun, two Sea Sparrow A/S quad missile launchers, two triple tube 324-mm Mk 32 torpedo launchers firing the Honeywell Mk 46 anti-submarine active/passive homing torpedo, and a single triple-barreled Limbo Mk.10 A/S mortar. Their twin "bunny-ear" funnels were a prominent identification feature. Apart from *Bras d'Or*, *Protecteur*, and *Preserver*, these were the first new warships built in Canada since the two *Annapolis* class DDHs were completed in 1964. The following photograph shows a view of *Iroquois* from astern, as originally commissioned.

These are considerably larger ships than the *St. Laurent*, *Restigouche*, *Mackenzie* and *Annapolis* class ships, displacing 3,551 tons compared with 2,263, 2,366, 2,380, and 2,400 tons, respectively. The *Tribals'* dimensions are 426' x 50' x 14', (length overall x beam x draught) compared with 366' x 42' x 13'-2". With the ability to carry two Sea King helicopters in addition to their own armament they are a good deal more of an antisubmarine threat than the earlier "steamers".

Iroquois as Originally Built

HMCS *Iroquois* as originally built, at anchor in Friar Roads, off the north shore of Campobello Island, New Brunswick, on July 4, 1982. She was here to participate in the celebrations for the 100th anniversary of the birth of Franklin D. Roosevelt, his summer cottage having been preserved on Campobello Island. Her large hangar, capable of carrying two helicopters, and her twin bunny-ear funnels are plainly visible, together with the variable depth sonar in her stern.

Her accommodation ladder is rigged on her starboard side, as is her boat boom on her port quarter, an inflatable boat being secured to it. She is dressed overall, with the United States flag at her masthead, in honour of Independence Day. Whether she is actually in American waters here is not certain. The international boundary cannot be any more than two miles away.

Her starboard Sea Sparrow missile launcher is visible, projecting outboard from her forward superstructure, with a missile in the launching position. Her starboard hangar door is open.

HMCS Iroquois

This close-up shows the 5-inch OTO Melara gun originally fitted in HMCS *Iroquois* and her sisters, as well as the front of her bridge. This gun could elevate to 85° and deliver a 32 kg shell to a range of 15 km (8 nautical miles), at a rate of 45 rounds per minute. Just abaft the gun is the SAM (surface to air) twin Raytheon Sea Sparrow quad launcher facility. These missiles had semi-active homing to 14.6 km (8 nm), and travelled at Mach 2.5, packing a 30 kg warhead. The ship carried 32 missiles.

These ships have a much more spacious bridge than their predecessors, with direct control of the main gas turbine engines on the bridge. The propulsion machinery originally consisted of two Pratt & Whitney FT4A2 gas turbines, developing 50,000 shp, giving a speed in excess of 29 knots. Two Pratt & Whitney FT12AH3 cruising gas turbines were also fitted, developing 7400 shp. These turbines drive two shafts with controllable pitch propellers.

This is the mast of the later *Tribal* class destroyer escort *Iroquois*, as she lies in HMC Dockyard, Halifax, in August 1988. She is flying the third substitute pennant, indicating her captain is ashore. There is considerably more highly sophisticated radar and electronic warfare equipment up the mast than seen in earlier ships. Since a warship can give her presence away very easily by using her radars or transmitting on her radios, a lot of work has been done on development of equipment to detect, locate and identify a warship by her radio or radar emissions.

There are two radar antennas visible in the picture, the upper being the surface search/navigation SMA SPQ 2D, I band antenna, and the lower, much larger antenna being the air search SPS 501 (LW03 antenna) D band antenna. Below these antennas, the spheres of the two Signaal WM22 I/J band fire control radars are prominent. These spherical housings each contain a combined antenna system comprising both a search and a tracking antenna, to give optimum azimuth coverage and fast, accurate target indication. Red and white barber pole stripes are painted around the pedestals of the fire control radars, continuing the custom of the "Barber Pole Squadron" established in the Second World War. For the really sharp-eyed, one of the ship's two air horns is mounted just above the barber pole stripes on the pedestal. The ship's badge is mounted on the front of the lower radar antenna platform. A wind speed and direction anemometer is mounted on the upper starboard yard. Just about everything else in the picture, apart from the top of the bunny-ear funnel at bottom right, is classified, but it is almost all concerned with communications, electronic warfare or electronic countermeasures. The squadron commander's pennant is barely visible at the top of the mast, and the first substitute pennant, flying from the starboard yard, can be seen immediately behind the larger radar's horn, indicating that he is ashore.

Canadian Warships

bear trap on the flight deck. It will be winched down until its projecting prong is securely caught and held by the bear trap. The bear trap can then be winched forward into the destroyer's hangar, once the helicopter's main rotor blades are folded. This arrangement allows helicopter operations even in quite rough seas.

Jane's Fighting Ships provides the following data about the Sea King helicopter:
Sikorsky CH-124A ASW and CH-124B Heltas Sea King, the latter dedicated to *Annapolis* and *Halifax* class ships.

Operational speed: 110 knots (203 km/h).

Service ceiling: 17,000 ft. (5,150 m).

Range: 410 nm (760 km).

Role: ASW, surface surveillance and support.

Sensors: APS-503 radar, sonobuoys, **ASQ-13** dipping sonar. The Heltas also has **MAD** (magnetic anomaly detector).

Weapons: Up to four Mk 46 torpedoes.

The 1965-66 edition of *Jane's All the World's Aircraft* provided additional technical information, the first of 36 similar helicopters having been delivered in May 1963:

The Sea King is a twin-engined amphibious all-weather anti-submarine helicopter with five-blade main and tail rotors. The main rotor blades are fitted with an automatic powered folding system. The fuselage is a boat hull of all-metal monocoque construction, with a fixed stabilizer on the starboard side of the tail section. The amphibious landing gear consists of two twin-wheel main units, which are retracted rearward hydraulically into stabilizing floats, and a non-retractable tailwheel. The boat hull and pop-out flotation bags in the stabilizing floats permit emergency operation from the water. The power plant originally consisted of two 1,250 shp General Electric T58-GE-8B shaft-turbine engines, though may have changed subsequently.

Dimensions, external:

Diameter of main rotor: 62 ft 0 in (18.90 m).

Diameter of tail rotor: 10 ft 4 in (3.15 m).

Length overall: 72 ft 8 in (22.15 m).

Width, rotors folded: 16 ft 4 in (4.98 m).

Height to top of rotor hub: 15 ft 6 in (4.72 m).

Weight: Normal take-off weight 18,044 lb (8,185 kg).

This *Tribal* class destroyer is capable of handling two Sea King helicopters, though not simultaneously, and the track for her other bear trap is visible at the bottom right of the picture.

Photo courtesy DND

Sea King Haul-Down

A Sea King helicopter is being hauled down onto a *Tribal's* flight deck in this photograph. It had previously lowered a cable, which the ship's helicopter handling crew connected to the haul-down cable. The helicopter is now hovering, pulling up against the tension in the haul-down cable issuing from the rectangular

HMCS Iroquois, TRUMPed

HMCS *Iroquois*, now TRUMPed, having had her Tribal Update and Modification Program refit, is seen entering Saint John harbour in June 1994. Her silhouette has changed considerably from her pre-TRUMP days, as she has exchanged her twin bunny-ear funnels for a single larger funnel, and has been given both a new gun and a new vertically-launched missile suite, as well as a new mast.

She shows some of the new equipment gained in the TRUMP refit. Just abaft her breakwater but unseen in the picture, is her Martin Marietta Mk 41 Vertical Launch System for 29 General Dynamics Standard SM-2MR Block III surface-to-air missiles (command/inertial guidance, semi-active radar homing to 73 km [40 nm] at Mach 2). Immediately abaft the missile suite is her new OTO Melara 3-inch (76-mm)/62 gun, mounted forward of her bridge (Super Rapid 85° elevation, 120 rounds/minute to 16 km [8.7 nm] weight of shell 6 kg). Looking further aft, directly over her bridge are her two STIR (Surveillance Tracking and Illumination Radar) 1.8 I/J band fire control radars. Mounted immediately abaft these, on its own pedestal, is the Signaal LW08 L band long range early warning air search radar. Its range performance against a two-square-meter target is about 145 nm. High atop the mast is her medium range search/navigation Signaal DA 08 E/F band radar. Its range performance against a two-square-metre target is almost 110 nm. Finally, atop the helicopter hangar, abaft the funnel, can be seen the white radar dome of her Phalanx Mk 15 gun (General Electric/General Dynamics 20-mm/76 6-barrelled, 3,000 rounds per minute combined to 0.8 nm). According to Thomas Lynch in "Trumping the Tribals: A Progress Report" in the 1986 edition of *Canada's Navy Annual*, "Phalanx comprises a pair of radar antennas which share a common Ku band (actually J band) transmitter for search and tracking and are mounted on the cradle of the M61A1 rotary barrelled Gatling gun....The Mk. 15 elevates from 25 to 80 degrees, the rate of elevation being 100 degrees per second with 100 degrees per second in slew rate." Phalanx is also known as "C-WIZ", for CIWS, or close-in weapons system.

One of her Sea King helicopters is visible on her flight deck, abaft the hangar. Underneath the flight deck can be seen the starboard triple 324-mm Mk 32 torpedo tube mounting which fires the Honeywell Mk 46 Mod 5 anti-submarine torpedo. The latter has active/passive homing with a range of 11 km (5.9 nm) at 40 kts. It carries a 44 kg warhead.

While keeping some of their anti-submarine armament, the TRUMP refit has given these ships a powerful anti-air warfare capability, something neglected in the Canadian Navy for much too long.

Iroquois in Saint John Harbour

This photograph of HMCS *Iroquois* gives a closer view from her starboard quarter. An Irving tug is alongside on her port quarter to assist her in berthing, as Saint John harbour has difficult tides and currents.

As previously mentioned, the *Iroquois* and her *Tribal* class sisters lost their bunny-ear twin funnels in their TRUMP refit, and gained a much larger, single funnel in exchange. There is a lot more to the funnel design than meets the eye. A warship can give her presence away not only by radar and radio transmissions, but also by the infra-red, or thermal, emissions, from her hot funnel gases, and so considerable work has been done to cool both these gases and the funnel outer surfaces to minimize her infra-red signature. Thomas G. Lynch's article, "Eliminating 'Hot-Spots': Canadian Naval IR Suppression Systems" in the May 1992 issue of *Navy International* explains:

The TRUMP IRSS (infra-red signature suppression) selected was based on the United States Navy's Boundary Layer Induced Stack Suppressor, or BLISS, as used in the Ticonderoga class. This device consisted of a 4-nozzle eductor followed by a mixing tube and entraining BLISS device for metal surface cooling. The eductor was used to add large quantities of cooling air for plume cooling. However the USN design did not meet TRUMP specifications in terms of view angle protection. As a result the DRES (Defence Research Establishment, Suffield) Ball diffusor section was mated with a lobed nozzle eductor, and the resulting device labelled the Eductor-Diffusor (E/D)..... Within this (funnel) structure, the effluent is fed though the E/D which consists (from bottom to top) of an ejector pump (4-lobed nozzle plus mixing tube) for entraining cool ambient air which cools the effluent plume, and a film-cooled diffusor which cools the stack surfaces themselves. Cool ambient-temperature air is drawn through a series of carefully baffled louvre systems on both sides of the new funnel structure.

There are actually six E/Ds in the funnel, two for the main FT-4 engines, two for the Allison 570KF cruise engines, and two for the main gas turbine/diesel generator sets.

Visible in her stern is the cutaway recess for her variable depth sonar. To starboard of the VDS cutaway are the twin openings for the two SLQ-25 Nixie acoustic torpedo decoys.

Though not obvious from the photographs, these ships had their FT12AH3 Pratt & Whitney cruise gas turbines (7,400 shp) replaced as part of TRUMP with the fuel-efficient General Motors Allison 570KF gas turbine (12,800 shp). They kept their original main engines, two Pratt & Whitney FT4A2 gas turbines, giving 50,000 shp. They have two shafts with controllable pitch propellers. The *Tribals* also lost their Mk. NC 10 Limbo, the ASW ahead-throwing mortar, in their TRUMP refit.

Photo courtesy SLt. Geoffrey Steed

HMCS Ville de Québec: The Halifax Class CPF

The *Halifax* class patrol frigate HMCS *Ville de Québec* is seen from HMCS *Montreal* at sea off Cape Breton Island, as both ships were proceeding to their commissioning ceremonies in Quebec City and Montreal respectively, in July 1994. These ships are arguably the most powerful warships Canada has ever possessed. Powered by two General Electric LM 2500 gas turbines, producing 47,494 hp (35.43 MW sustained) or a SEMT-Pielstick 20 PA6 V 280 cruise diesel engine developing 8,800 hp (6.48 MW sustained), they have a speed in excess of 29 knots. The gas turbines and diesel drive two controllable pitch propellers through two main gear boxes and a cross-connect gearbox. The following armament is carried:

Missiles:
SSM (surface-to-surface missiles) 8 McDonnell Douglas Harpoon Block 1C (2 quadruple) launchers, active radar homing to 130 km (70 nm) at 0.9 Mach, 227 kg warhead.
SAM (surface-to-air missiles) 2 Raytheon Sea Sparrow Mk 48 octuple vertical launchers, semi-active radar homing to 14.6 km (8 nm) at 2.5 Mach, 39 kg warhead, 16 missiles.

Guns:
1 Bofors 57-mm/70 Mk 2, 77° elevation, 220 rounds per minute to 17 km (9 nm), weight of shell 2.4 kg.
1 GE/GDC 20-mm Vulcan Phalanx Mk 15 Mod 1, anti-missile, 3,000 rounds per minute (6 barrels combined) to 1.5 km.
6 50-calibre machine guns.

Torpedoes:
4 324-mm Mk 32 Mod 9 (2 twin) tubes, 24 Honeywell Mk 46 Mod 5, anti-submarine, active/passive homing to 11 km (5.9 nm) at 40 kts, warhead 44 kg

Helicopter:
1 CH-124A ASW or 1 CH-124B Heltas Sea King

Similar to that of the TRUMPed Tribals, the funnel incorporates infra-red signature suppression facilities known as the DRES Ball for the main gas turbines, and 'Cheesegraters' for the cruise diesel and generator sets. Again quoting from Lynch's May 1992 article:

The DRES Ball provides IR suppression for all angles of view and consists of a film-cooled outer duct surrounding a convectively and film-cooled optical block centre body and a film-cooled diffuser. The centre "ball" is used to block any view down into the exhaust duct, thereby eliminating the direct line of sight of the hot ducting. All visible metal surfaces are either cooled by convection methods or film-cooled...To date (and in the opinion of several of the world's navies), the DRES Ball is a world beater in stack effluent IR suppression and should remain so for at least the next generation of NATO warship designs.

HMCS Ville de Québec

The *Halifax* class patrol frigate HMCS *Ville de Québec* is shown secured alongside in Saint John in June 1994. The range of the tide in Saint John, being on the Bay of Fundy, is some 20 feet, so the duty watch of a ship has to be alert to ensure that the berthing hawsers remain correctly tensioned, and that the brow can be negotiated safely.

This class of ship has only a single anchor, positioned dead centre in her bow. Apparently there was some difficulty originally with it coming home, as its stock is only a few degrees above the horizontal when it is stowed, but this has been overcome. Her Bofors 57-mm/70 gun is visible on the fo'c'sle, just forward of the bridge. It is designed to deal with both air and surface targets. The round object above the bridge is her K/L-band Signaal VM25 STIR (Surveillance, Tracking and Illuminating Radar), range 140 km (76 nm) for a one square metre target. It provides fire control data for the Sea Sparrow missiles and the Bofors 57-mm gun. Directly above the STIR radar is her Raytheon AN/SPS-49(V)5 two-dimensional C/D-band surveillance radar, capable of detecting a 2-metre target at 457 km and tracking 250 targets simultaneously. The large vertical dipole antenna mounted on the platform projecting out to starboard from the mast is the Line of Sight (LOS) antenna for her RT-5073 V1/WSC UHF transceivers used for line-of-sight and satellite (ship-shore-ship) communications for voice, radio-assisted teletype (RATT), and modulated CW emissions. Just above the platform projecting to starboard from the mast is her Ericsson's Sea Giraffe HC 150 G/H-band surveillance radar, which provides cover against low-flying aircraft and missiles in conditions of heavy 'clutter' to a range of 100 km (55 nm). The antenna at the extreme top of the mast is her URN 25 IFF Mk XII Tacan, for helicopter homing.

Far less technical in nature, two pairs of pneumatic fenders are hanging over her side ready for placement to protect her from scraping against the jetty as the tide rises or falls. Her doubled-up fore back spring is taut due to the influence of the strong current from the Saint John River flowing through the harbour, as is her doubled-up head rope as it leads through the bullring at her bow. Many are the hands, improperly ashore in foreign ports, who have attempted to come back on board undetected by climbing these hawsers at night!

HMCS Toronto

The Canadian Patrol Frigate (CPF) HMCS *Toronto* is seen in this aerial view from astern. The hollow square on the fo'c'sle, in yellow paint, defines the dump area for helicopter vertical replenishment or hoist transfers. It is bisected by the anchor cable leading forward to the hawse pipe in the bow. The Bofors 57-mm/70 gun is just forward of the bridge, surrounded by the breakwater to protect it from seas breaking over the fo'c'sle.

Further aft, the two gas turbine exhausts are visible in the top of the funnel. Immediately outboard of the funnel, on the upper deck, the port Sea Sparrow octuple vertical launcher array can be seen, though at the time this photograph was taken the missiles themselves were not fitted. The starboard side launcher can be seen just to the right of the after face of the funnel. Immediately abaft the port launcher, looking rather like a deck chair frame in this view, the port Harpoon missile quadruple launcher can be seen, though again, the missiles themselves are not installed. The helicopter hangar is immediately abaft the funnel, and the after STIR radar can be seen atop its pedestal at the forward end of the hangar. The 20-mm Vulcan Phalanx gun is at the after end of the hangar on its starboard side. The "glass house" high up on the port side of the after end of the hangar, overlooking the flight deck, is the Flight Deck Co-ordinator's position. "FLYCO" is responsible for co-ordination of activities if the ship is unlucky enough to have a crash-on-deck. The other glass house, projecting just above the flight deck on the starboard side, is the Landing Signals Officer's compartment. The LSO is responsible to the Officer of the Watch for all flying operations. He looks after landings, launches, fuelling, crew changes and anything else which occurs on the flight deck. The lines running from the hangar door most of the way aft along the flight deck are the slots for the bear trap helicopter hauldown device. Numerous 20-man inflatable life raft canisters can be seen around the forward superstructure, the helicopter hangar, and at the stern.

Photo courtesy DND

Canadian Warships

The Halifax Class: A Modern Warship

contributed by Commander Laverne Fleck

One joins the Navy dreaming of going to sea in sleek ships and of one day commanding your own. I was most fortunate to do just that. My two years as captain of HMCS *Toronto* were exhilarating, challenging, at times demanding and always rewarding. I feel now, as I did that day when I first stepped on board as captain, a sense of awe, privilege, and pride; and, as all

Photo courtesy DND

captains do, a belief that your ship and crew are quite simply the best.

The Canadian Patrol Frigate, or more properly the *Halifax* class frigate after the lead ship, since its delivery to the Canadian Navy in the early 1990s, has proven to be one of the most versatile, general purpose warships in the world. Since entering service, these ships have served operationally in support of the United Nations in both the Adriatic Sea and the Persian Gulf, worked with NATO, conducted several daring rescues of ships in distress, as well as patrolled Canadian waters in support of the Department of Fisheries and Oceans to protect our fishing industry and the RCMP to counter drug smuggling. The *Halifax* class is a frigate in the traditional sense of the word. It is fully capable of operating with other ships in the escort role or working independently in a surveillance role at considerable distance from the main part of the fleet or support ships. Several factors contribute to this versatility. The ship has excellent speed, fine sea keeping capabilities and outstanding endurance. For example, it can cross the Atlantic and return handily without refuelling. A second key attribute of a frigate is an excellent surveillance capability. The *Halifax* class with its modern radars, electronic warfare equipment, state of the art sonars (both hull mounted and towed array), and its own helicopter is able to provide surveillance above, on and under the water of an area 100 nautical miles around the ship - an area considerably larger than Lake Ontario. The *Halifax* class also has excellent self-defence capability, the final attribute of a frigate. The Sea Sparrow missile, the Bofors 57-mm gun and the Phalanx Close-In-Weapon System (CIWS) provide layered anti-air Defence. The Harpoon missile provides a long range anti-ship capability and torpedoes, both ship launched and helicopter launched, provide anti-submarine capability. In addition, the ship has a full electronic warfare suite including a radar jammer, chaff rockets and infra-red decoys to assist in anti-ship missile Defence.

Perhaps the biggest change between a World War Two ship and today's modern warship is the operations room. It is from the operations room that the ship is fought, and it is here, not the bridge, where the captain spends most of his time during operations. Information from all the ship's sensors (radars, sonars, electronic warfare equipment) is fed directly to the operations room where it is displayed on computer screens and passed automatically via data link to other ships in company. Similarly, information received from other ships is automatically displayed on your own ship's computers. Without question, the most demanding task of a captain and his combat team is to sort through the volumes of available information, assimilate the real picture and be prepared to react quickly to any threat. The speed of modern weapons systems means that reaction times are now measured in seconds.

If 'fighting' a modern warship is the most demanding task of a captain, 'driving' that ship is the most exhilarating (read fun). In this regard, the *Halifax* class is second to none. The ship has a very flexible propulsion system. In naval nomenclature, the system is known as CODOG, Combined Diesel or Gas. Two General Electric LM2500 gas turbines combine to generate 50,000 horsepower to propel the ship to just over 30 knots (up to 26 knots on one gas turbine). A fuel efficient Pielstick diesel engine of 8,800 horsepower allows the ship to cruise for greatly extended ranges at up to 19 knots. Unique to the *Halifax* class is a cross-connect gearbox which permits either of the gas turbines or the Pielstick diesel to drive both shafts. A Canadian developed Integrated Machinery Control System (IMCS) provides computerized control of the entire engineering system. Switching from one propulsion system to another is simple and quick. For example, transferring from the diesel to full power with two gas turbines takes only 90 seconds.

The *Halifax* class is incredibly manoeuverable. It can accelerate from stopped in the water to 30 knots in 60 seconds and stop from 30 knots in less than 500 metres. At 30 knots and maximum helm, the ship will heel over close to 20 degrees while turning in a 600 metres diameter circle. The real beauty is that the power is there for immediate use. The gas turbines are robust and perfectly comfortable at full power, and IMCS allows you to go to full power quickly with complete control. A 'Full Speed' order is no longer considered an emergency order but rather to be used whenever the situation warrants. The readily available power, the precise speed control, and the rapid rudder reaction at speed combine to make ship handling at sea a real treat. The *Halifax* class can be brought alongside a replenishment ship quickly and with precision. The ship handles very well alongside the replenishment ship, and station keeping is easily accomplished in all but the most severe of weather conditions.

The *Halifax* class rides very well in all sea states. Most would categorize the motion of the ship as 'stiff'. For those familiar with the rhythmic rolling motion of our former ships, the more unpredictable, quicker motion of the *Halifax* class takes some getting used to. In medium seas of three to five metres, the ship cuts through the waves easily and high speed can be maintained. In heavy seas, pitching motion must be watched closely as the rather short fo'c'sle has a tendency to dig in causing waves to break against the bridge, potentially damaging equipment on the bridge top. That said, *Toronto* was in a storm off Newfoundland in 12- to 14-metre seas. By keeping the seas 20 degrees off the bow, the ship was able to maintain 8 to 10 knots while riding comfortably (less than 20-degree rolls) and sustaining no damage.

Handling the *Halifax* class in the narrow confines of a harbour can be a challenge. One must always be cognisant of the strengths and weaknesses of a gas turbine, variable pitch twin screw ship with a single rudder. On the plus side, as mentioned previously, the *Halifax* class has very quick acceleration and deceleration. From five knots, the ship can be stopped in 100 metres, less than one ship length, with only moderate astern power. Secondly, the ship handles very well if at least five knots is made through the water, either ahead or astern. However, at less than three knots the ship handles sluggishly and maintaining a heading can be difficult in windy conditions. The *Halifax* class also does not turn well at rest; again, primarily because of the hydrodynamics of variable pitch propellers and a single rudder. The wind is also much more of a consideration than it was with our previous ships. The *Halifax* class drifts with the wind at about a 1:12 ratio; that is, a 12-knot wind on the beam will cause a lateral drift of one knot. Secondly, the ship wants to lie beam to the wind when stopped or proceeding at low speed. This causes two problems: turning at rest in winds greater than 20 to 25 knots is very problematic and, with the wind on the bow or quarter, the ship has a distinct tendency to shear to put the wind on the beam as it slows during a jetty approach. When driving a *Halifax* class, one therefore uses speed and power to advantage. An approach to a jetty is fast, typically five knots until 100 metres from the berth. As one captain advised me when I took command, "If you don't scare yourself during a jetty approach, you probably took your speed off too early." The requirement for tug assistance in berthing and departing is much more common now than with previous classes of ships and is almost automatic in winds of greater than 20 knots.

Regardless of its technical sophistication, its modern equipment or its operating characteristics, the heart and soul of the ship is its ship's company. Undeniably, the most rewarding part of command is working with the men and women who sail in her. The *Halifax* class ship's company at 225, including the helicopter detachment, is small for a ship of its size. Automation and computers have made this possible, but there is no room for slack. Each member of the ship's company has a role to play and, quite literally, a chair to fill. Each must be highly trained and able to do his or her job with a minimum of supervision. There are very few bunks onboard for trainees so we rely much more heavily on ashore trainers and simulators than ever before. The small crew size makes for a tightly knit ship's company but also means that traditional ship's husbandry and storing ship cannot be left only for the ordinary seamen. All ranks, including officers and petty officers, are expected to lend a hand for manpower intensive evolutions. In my experience, this was never a problem. The ship's company were incredibly proud of their ship and eager to get the job done. Or as someone put it to me, "Before, we had to train hard and work hard to make up for our poor equipment; now we have to train hard and work hard to keep up with our equipment." It is a pleasant change indeed.

Laverne Fleck, Commander, Commanding Officer, HMCS *Toronto*, 1995-1997

HMCS Preserver and HMCS Iroquois

The operational support ship HMCS *Preserver* and the TRUMPed *Tribal* class destroyer (DDH) *Iroquois* berthed outboard are shown alongside in Saint John in November 1995.

Preserver and her sistership *Protecteur* followed on from *Provider*. These ships have an 8,380 tons light, 24,700 tons full load displacement, and have a length of 564 feet. They have a range of 4,100 miles at 20 knots, and can carry 14,590 tons of fuel, 400 tons of aviation fuel, 1,048 tons of dry cargo, and 1,250 tons of ammunition. They can carry three Sea King helicopters. They have two GE/GDC 20-mm/76 6-barrelled Vulcan Phalanx Mk 15 guns and 6 12.7-mm machine guns. One of the Phalanx guns can be seen mounted above *Preserver's* bridge. Like *Provider*, these ships have four fuelling positions. *Preserver* has rigged ratguards on her berthing hawsers, and her port anchor is down, likely as security against the ferocious currents in Saint John harbour. *Preserver* and *Protecteur* have twin funnels, one on each side of their helicopter hangar. The starboard funnel is visible in the photograph. Both ships originally were fitted with "bow-chaser" 3-inch-50 twin gun mountings in the bow, but these have been removed.

Iroquois' OTO Melara 3-in.(76-mm)/62 gun is visible, mounted just forward of her bridge. One of her two STIR radars(Surveillance Tracking and Illumination Radar) is immediately above the port side of the bridge, and the large Signaal LW08 L band long range early warning air search radar is mounted on its own barber-pole striped pedestal, just forward of the mast, above the bridge. Close to the top of the mast, her medium range search/navigation Signaal DA 08 E/F band radar can be seen. Finally, her starboard anchor pocket is visible in her bow. This was originally closed by a hinged door, very much like that in the *St. Laurent*, *Restigouche*, *Mackenzie* and *Annapolis* class ships, but it was found to be too troublesome, and was discarded.

HMCSm Grilse

HMCSm *Grilse* was the ex-US *Balao* class USS *Burrfish*, a radar picket submarine, and prior to that, the USS *Amilio*. Completed on September 14, 1943, she was loaned to the Royal Canadian Navy in 1960 for five years with the option of renewal. Having a displacement of 1,816 tons on the surface, and 2,425 tons submerged, and a length of 311½ feet, she carried six 21-inch torpedo tubes, and was based in Esquimalt for use in anti-submarine warfare training. Her 6,500 hp diesels could drive her on the surface at 20 knots, and achieve a range of 12,000 miles at 10 knots. Her electric motors could develop 4,610 shp, giving her a submerged speed of 10 knots. Her complement was 7 officers, and 72 men, with additional accommodation for 2 officers and 9 men.

Grilse was succeeded by HMCSm *Rainbow*. Julie Robinson writes in *Through a Canadian Periscope: The Story of the Canadian Submarine Service*:

After *Rainbow* arrived [she was commissioned into the Canadian Navy on 2 December, 1968], *Grilse* never sailed again for the Canadian Navy, even though there were two years to run on her second contract and she had been refitted [at a cost of $1.2 million in early 1967]. As the navy had managed to get *Rainbow* by convincing the politicians that the older submarine was unsafe, *Grilse* languished alongside. Some of her more modern gear was transferred to *Rainbow* during her modernization, but had to be returned when the American auditors reminded Canada that *Grilse* had to be operational when she reverted to the USN. In September 1969 *Grilse* went back home to be used for target practice and now rests on the bottom of the Pacific west of San Francisco, fully equipped...*Grilse* had provided value for money as a tame submarine and had the honour of restarting the Canadian Submarine Service after a gap of nearly 50 years. She re-established the tradition, initiated a rebirth of pride in submarines, and provided a necessary example of what a submarine could do to the top brass and politicians in Ottawa. If it had not been for the *Grilse*, the navy would have found it even more difficult than it was to acquire three new operational submarines in the 1960s.

Photo courtesy DND

HMCSm Rainbow

HMCSm *Rainbow* was the ex-US *Tench* class USS *Argonaut*. According to *Jane's Fighting Ships* she was built by the Navy Yard, Portsmouth, New Hampshire, and completed on January 15, 1945. She was purchased in December 1968 by Canada as a replacement for *Grilse*, being commissioned on December 2, 1968, and based in Esquimalt for anti-submarine training until December 31, 1974. With a displacement of 1,800 tons on the surface, and 2,500 tons submerged, and a length of 311 feet, she carried ten 21-inch torpedo tubes. Her 6,500 hp diesel engines gave her a speed of 20 knots on the surface, and her 4,610 hp electric motors 10 knots submerged. With a complement of 8 officers and 74 men, she had a range of 12,000 miles on the surface at 10 knots. Julie Robinson writes that over two years after she was decommissioned, *Rainbow* was towed to Portland, Oregon, where she was broken up.

Photo courtesy DND

HMCSm Okanagan and HMCSm Ojibwa

Both photographs on this page show Canadian *Oberon* class patrol submarines in the harbour of Saint John, New Brunswick. The picture on the left was taken in July 1990, and is of HMCSm *Okanagan*, while that on the right was taken in March 1996, and is of HMCSm *Ojibwa*. *Ojibwa* is secured alongside the Pugsley pier, while *Okanagan* has just slipped her mooring lines and is going astern, in preparation for leaving harbour. The bow planes are in their vertical stowed position in both views, one or two periscopes or masts are projecting above the conning tower or "sail" of each boat, and the sonar domes of each boat are prominent at the bow. *Ojibwa* had undergone her Submarine Operational Update Project (SOUP) which gave her more modern sonar and fire control equipment.

Ojibwa, the first of these three *Oberon* class boats, was laid down on September 27, 1962, launched on February 29, 1964, and commissioned on September 23, 1965. She was paid off on May 21, 1998. Quite an age for a submarine! Her sister, *Okanagan*, paid off on September 8, 1998. Only *Onondaga* is still in commission. However, it is essential that Canada have a submarine with which to train its anti-submarine forces, and this boat continues to give good service. It was announced in April 1998 that Canada will lease four *Upholder* class submarines from Britain. These are conventionally powered "boats". It will be interesting to see how long it takes for them to be turned over to Canada, and commissioned. *Onondaga* is expected to continue in service until then.

Jane's Fighting Ships gives the following particulars of Canada's *Oberons*:

Displacement, tons: 2,030 surfaced;
2,410 submerged.

Dimensions, feet (metres):
295.2 x 26.5 x 18 (90 x 8.1 x 5.5).

Main machinery: Diesel-electric: 2 ASR 16 VVS.ASR1 diesels: 3,680 hp (2.74MW);
2 AEI motors: 6,000 hp (4.48 MW); 2 shafts.

Speed, knots: 12 surfaced;
17 dived, 10 snorting.
Range, miles 9,000 surfaced at 12 kts.

Complement: 65 (7 officers).

Torpedoes: 6 21-in (533-mm) bow tubes.
20 Goulds Mk 48 Mod 4, dual purpose; active/passive homing to 50 km (27 nm)/38 km (21 nm) at 40/55 kts; warhead 267 kg.

Countermeasures: ESM;
Sperry Guardian Star; radar warning.

Weapons Control: Loral Librascope TFCS with Sperry UYK 20 computer.

Radars: Navigation: Kelvin Hughes Type 1006 or Furuno 1831 (Onondaga); I-band.

Sonars: Plessey Triton Type 2051, hull-mounted passive/active search and attack; medium frequency. BAC Type 2007 AC; flank array, passive search; long range, low frequency. BQG 501 Sperry Micropuffs; passive ranging. Hermes Electronics/MUSL towed array; passive low frequency.

Photo courtesy SLt. Geoffrey Steed

Photo courtesy D. Perkins

The Royal Navy's Upholder Class

The Canadian Government announced on April 6, 1998, that Canada will lease all four of the Royal Navy's mothballed *Upholder* class submarines for a period of eight years, at a price of $610-million. While the arrangements are not finalized, and the submarines not yet in Canadian waters, they are included here.

HMSm *Upholder*, the first of the class of four, was ordered from Vickers Shipbuilding & Engineering (VSEL), Barrow-in-Furness, on November 2, 1983, and a further three were ordered on January 2, 1986. *Upholder* was commissioned on June 9, 1990, and *Unseen*, *Ursula*, and *Unicorn* followed on June 7, 1991, May 8, 1992, and June 25, 1993, respectively, the last three being built by Cammell Laird, Birkenhead (VSEL). *Upholder* and *Unseen* were placed in reserve in April 1994 as a money-saving expedient, and the other two were reported in *Jane's* as being expected to pay off by the end of that year. *Jane's* was no longer showing these vessels following its 1994-95 edition.

Upholder is the second British submarine to bear the name, the first being commanded by LCdr M.D. Wanklyn VC, RN. Before being lost on her 25th patrol in April 1942, having operated in the Mediterranean for 16 months, she had sunk three U-boats and one destroyer, damaged one cruiser and one destroyer, and sunk or damaged 19 Axis supply ships totalling 119,000 tons. *Unseen* and *Ursula* also had predecessors bearing the same names in the 44-boat "U" Class launched between 1937 and 1943.

Canadian Warships

The present *Upholders*, like their predecessors, are diesel-powered. Armament details are subject to change as they are adapted to suit Canadian requirements. These submarines should serve Canada's need for many years to come. *Jane's* gives their particulars as follows:

Displacement, tons: 2168 surfaced; 2455 dived
Dimensions, feet (metres): 230.6 x 25 x 17.7 (70.3 x 7.6 x 5.5)

Main machinery: Diesel-electric; 2 Paxman Valenta 16SZ diesels 3620 hp (2.7 MW) sustained; 2 GEC alternators; 2.8 MW; 1 GEC motor; 5400 hp (4 MW); 1 shaft.

Speed, knots: 12 surfaced; 20 dived; 12 snorting

Range, miles: 8000 at 8 knots snorting

Complement: 47 (7 officers)
Structure: Single skinned NQ1 high tensile steel hull, tear dropped shape 9:1 ratio, 5 man lock-out chamber in fin. This is the first time that the Valenta diesel has been fitted in submarines. Fitted with elastomeric acoustic tiles. Diving depth, greater than 200 m (650 ft). Fitted with Pilkington optronics **CK 35** search and **CH 85** attack optronic periscopes.

Photo courtesy UK Ministry of Defense

HMCS Yukon and Minesweepers

Four *Bay* class minesweepers, the nearest one being HMCS *Chaleur*, are berthed on *Yukon* in this photograph taken in HMC Dockyard, Esquimalt, in the summer of 1993. *Yukon* appears to be secured alongside the Seaward Defence Jetty, on the west side of Dockyard. All these ships were nearing the end of their lives at this time, and though the minesweepers all appear to be flying their third substitute pennants, indicating their commanding officers are ashore, there is little sign of life on board *Yukon*.

Photo courtesy SLt. Geoffrey Steed

Photo courtesy SLt. Geoffrey Steed

HMCS Chignecto

The *Bay* class former minesweeper HMCS *Chignecto* is seen in the summer of 1993. Destroyers or destroyer escorts are not big ships, but minesweepers are a great deal smaller! By this stage in their life, the minesweepers had landed their minesweeping gear and were being used mainly for junior officer ship handling training.

These 164-foot-long, wooden-hulled vessels had aluminum frames and decks. They displaced 370 tons standard, and 470 tons full load. Powered by two GM 12-278A diesels, driving two shafts, they had a speed of 15 knots and a range of 4,500 miles at 11 knots. Her anchor is a Danforth type, unlike the stockless type carried in larger warships. Her surface search Racal Decca I-band radar antenna is visible on the mast above the open bridge. Her two derricks, one on either side of her funnel, have survived from her minesweeping days, but the after deckhouse has replaced the winch and associated gear for handling her sweeps. Her inflatable boat is lying alongside, at the foot of a Jacob's ladder.

HMCS Cape Breton

HMCS *Cape Breton* is seen with her starboard anchor "a-cockbill", ready for letting go. Her sister ship, *Cape Scott*, was almost identical. They were escort maintenance ships. *The Ships of Canada's Naval Forces 1910-1993* gives a capsule history of these ships:

These modified *Fort* type cargo ships were launched at Vancouver in 1944 as HMS *Beachy Head* and *Flamborough Head*. The latter continued in service with the RN after the war, but *Beachy Head* was turned over to the Royal Netherlands Navy in 1947 as repair ship *Vulkaan*. In 1950 she was returned to the RN and resumed her original name until 1952, when she was transferred to the RCN and, in 1953, renamed *Cape Scott*. She lay alongside her sister, *Cape Breton*, at Halifax for some years, providing supplementary workshops and classroom facilities until *Cape Breton* was transferred to the west coast in 1958. After a refit at Saint John, *Cape Scott* was at last commissioned on January 28, 1959, to serve at Halifax until paid off into reserve on July 1, 1970. In 1972 she was redesignated Fleet Maintenance Group (Atlantic), but was sold when the group moved ashore in 1975 and left under tow in 1978 to be broken up in Texas.

Flamborough Head was also acquired from the RN in 1952, and renamed *Cape Breton* upon commissioning on January 31, 1953. She served at Halifax until August 25, 1958, as repair ship and training establishment for technical apprentices. Converted to escort maintenance ship at Esquimalt, she was commissioned there on November 16, 1959, for service on the west coast. On February 10, 1964, *Cape Breton* was paid off into reserve, but since 1972 she has functioned as a towed mobile support facility and accommodation vessel at Esquimalt, designated Fleet Maintenance Group (Pacific).

Both ships were equipped with a helicopter landing platform, a decompression chamber for the ship's divers, engineering, electrical and electronic repair shops, diesel engine repair shop, battery shop, sheet metal shop, welding shop, pipe and copper smith's shop, plate shop and blacksmith's shop. Each ship contained an eight-berth hospital, large sick bay, operating theatre, X-ray room, small medical laboratory, dental clinic and dental laboratory.

Sister ships *Berry Head* and *Rame Head*, also built by Burrard Drydock Company at Vancouver, had long careers in the RN. *Berry Head* served until 1988, and was towed to Turkey for breaking up, arriving in March 1990. *Rame Head* became a Royal Marines training ship in December 1991.

Photo courtesy DND

Canadian Warships

HMCS Anticosti

The Minesweeper Auxiliary (MSA) HMCS *Anticosti* is underway in Halifax harbour in this photograph, off HMC Dockyard, with either the *Preserver* or *Protecteur* and the Angus L. Macdonald Bridge in the background. She was previously the *Jean Tide*, a former offshore towing/supply vessel, Ice Class 3, suitable for navigation in light ice, according to *Jane's Fighting Ships*. Displacing 1,076 tons full load, she is 191 feet long, and with four Nohab Polar SF 16RS diesels, totalling 4,600 hp, her two shafts give her a speed of 13.5 knots and a range of 12,000 miles at 13 knots. She has mechanical sweep gear. She has two Racal Decca I-band radars for navigation, and side scan towed high frequency variable depth sonar (VDS). She has a complement of 18, including five officers, made up of a mix of Regulars and Reservists. Both *Anticosti* and her sister *Moresby* have a triple drum towing winch of 300,000-lb pull capacity. *Anticosti* was fitted with astern refuelling in mid-1995.

Photo courtesy DND

HMCS Porte St. Jean

The Gate Vessel (YMG) HMCS *Porte St. Jean* is seen underway, and, like *Anticosti* is also flying her call sign in a flag hoist.

Of trawler design, these multi-purpose vessels were used for operating the gates in anti-submarine booms, and as fleet auxiliaries and anti-submarine netlayers for opening and closing entrances to defended harbours. They were also capable of being fitted for minesweeping. *Jane's Fighting Ships* gives the particulars of these vessels as follows:

Displacement, tons: 429 full load

Dimensions, feet 125.5 x 26.3 x 13

Guns: 1 - 40-mm AA

Main Engines: Diesel; A/C Electric; one shaft; 600 bhp=11 knots

Complement 3 officers; 20 ratings

Photo courtesy DND

HMCS Kingston

HMCS *Kingston*, the lead ship of the *Kingston* class of Maritime Coastal Defence Vessels (MCDV), proceeds to sea from HMC Dockyard, Halifax. Georges Island with its lighthouse and part of the Halifax waterfront are in the background.

The Canadian Navy's Internet Web page provides an excellent description of this class (http://www.dnd.ca/navy/marcom/cdnnavy.html):

> The primary mission of the *Kingston* class is coastal surveillance and patrol. This will involve a wide variety of duties, including: general naval operations and exercises; search and rescue; and support to other government departments in the areas of law enforcement, resource protection and fisheries and environmental monitoring. In addition, interchangeable modular payloads will provide a mine countermeasures (MCM) capability including mine sweeping and mine hunting.
>
> Four state-of-the-art route survey (RS) payloads will produce high quality sidescan sonar imagery of the ocean bottom. The analysed information will be used for route mapping, detection and classification of mine-like objects and the optimisation of ocean route planning. Two RS payloads will be assigned to each coast.
>
> Two mechanical minesweeping systems (MMS) will be capable of providing a minesweeping countermeasure against modern buoyant (moored) mines. The MMS will be capable of conducting single ship as well as team sweeping operations. These payloads will be assigned to the East Coast.
>
> A single bottom object inspection (BOI) payload will provide the capability of inspecting mine-like objects on the sea bed using sonar and video sensors mounted on a remote operated vehicle (ROV). This payload will be capable of supporting port inspection or explosive ordnance disposal (EOD) diving teams for mine clearance or EOD tasks. This payload will be assigned to the West Coast.
>
> MCDVs will be crewed by naval reservists and two regular force naval electronic technicians with a minimum crew of 31 for coastal surveillance and patrol, to a maximum crew of 36 required for route survey operations. This will allow the size of vessel crews to be adjusted to meet operational requirements, while at the same time, maximizing service opportunities for reservists.
>
> Six MCDVs will be assigned to each coast and will be based in Halifax and Esquimalt, B.C. During the ice-free months (May - Nov) each year, up to four of the East Coast vessels will be based in Quebec City and deploy to the Great Lakes/St. Lawrence River area.

Photo courtesy DND

Photo courtesy DND

HMCS Cormorant

This is a view of the fleet diving support ship HMCS *Cormorant*. According to the Canadian Navy's web page,

Cormorant is a 75-metre, 2,350-tonne ship with a crew of 82, a recompression chamber and equipment to support scuba and mixed-gas diving plus the mini-submarine SDL-1, which could carry five people to depths of 600 metres.

Cormorant, a former Italian trawler, was bought by Canada in 1975 and underwent extensive modification prior to being commissioned in November 1978. Two years later, she became the first navy ship to have a mixed-gender crew. Although *Cormorant* is being retired, the navy retains the ability to inspect, identify and retrieve objects from the seabed thanks to remote-controlled, unmanned submersibles that will operate at lower cost and with less risk to human safety from *Kingston* class ships on both the Atlantic and Pacific coasts.

Over the years, *Cormorant's* capabilities have been used to locate or retrieve everything from submerged aircraft to multi-million-dollar caches of illegal drugs. *Cormorant's* crew and submersible videotaped and plugged leaks in the sunken oil barge *Irving Whale* off Prince Edward Island and helped recover the ship's bell from the wreck of the *Edmund Fitzgerald* in Lake Superior. The ship has also taken scientists to the seabeds of the Atlantic and Caribbean as well as the Great Lakes for a wide range of research projects.

She was paid off on July 2, 1997, and subsequently sold.

Yard Auxiliary Gate Vessels

These two so-called YAGs, Yard Auxiliary Gate vessels, wooden-hulled training vessels, had spent the night here tied up alongside a jetty in Browning Harbour, on Pender Island in the Gulf Islands between Victoria and Vancouver in April 1996. Present day frigates and destroyers are much too expensive to use for officer cadet navigation training, and these vessels, together with the wooden-hulled minesweepers, have taken the place of the frigates of the sixties for pilotage training.

In times of budget restraint, these vessels have served the navy well in providing relatively inexpensive training platforms for young naval officers in the basics of navigation and collision avoidance. The candidates complete theoretical instruction in a classroom followed by two or three weeks of application in these vessels. The cruises consist of passages through the Gulf Islands to refine the navigation skills of junior officers. As these vessels are small and slow, most of the passages are conducted during the day and, as much as possible, away from the deep sea shipping traffic lanes. At night, the vessels go alongside in such exotic ports as Browning Harbour and Cowichan Bay! This gives the crew and the young officers a chance to unwind, as well as time to prepare for the following day's passages. Each passage could take up to two or three hours to plan, and just as long to execute. The permanent crew of each of these vessels consists of only two persons, a stoker and an assistant. The captain is usually the divisional training officer, and the positions of officer-of-the-watch, navigator, helmsman, lookout, lifebuoy sentry, and cook are all manned by the trainees.

These vessels are 75'3" in length, with a beam of 18'3", and a maximum displacement of 70 tons. Eight are still in service on the West Coast. They were built in the fifties by a yard on Gabriola Island. They have two shafts, each powered by a diesel, which allows them to achieve a maximum of 11 knots. Navigation is primitive in bad weather as the radar is a very old Sperry which provides a relative picture only. Pilotage is conducted from atop the wheelhouse position giving a good all around view. Unfortunately, the only protection afforded the charts during foul weather is a hooded chart table which is not always effective, depending on the angle of rainfall. The after house has been transformed to provide accommodations for trainees as well as a working space; and the regular crew, the captain and sometimes female cadets are berthed forward under the wheelhouse.

HMCS Cape Breton, HMCS Restigouche and HMCS Kootenay

A visit to HMC Dockyard, Esquimalt, in October 1998 revealed a number of warships lying there. In addition to the modern *Halifax* class patrol frigate *Calgary*, berthed at the fuelling jetty, there was quite a collection of de-commissioned ships awaiting disposal. *Annapolis* was lying at the most southerly jetty, facing seawards, looking quite derelict without her radar antennas. One of the *Porte* class gate vessels was along the north side of this same jetty, along with several minesweepers, only two of which were still in commission, and not likely to remain so for long. At the most northerly jetty lay *Cape Breton* inboard, *Restigouche*, and *Kootenay* outboard, as pictured here. They had already had significant pieces of equipment removed: *Cape Breton* was missing her anchors, *Restigouche* was missing her 3-inch-70 gun's director from above the bridge, and *Kootenay* had already had her 3-inch-70 gun turret removed. Both DDEs had lost their satellite communications antennas from their mounting brackets above their bridge wings. It was a rather sad sight to see such fine ships awaiting their fates. The small ship stern-on at the left of the photograph is the diving tender HMCS *Sooke*, one of four *Sechelt* class auxiliaries. She can support diving operations to a depth of 80 meters.

This photograph is a fitting ending to this book, as it shows *Cape Breton*, the oldest surviving Canadian naval vessel, launched in Vancouver in 1944, together with two of the last steam-powered Improved *Restigouche* class ships, the lives of these three ships totalling approximately (54+40+39) 133 years from date of launch.

CANADIAN WARSHIPS

APPENDIX

Appendix A: Ships by Class, with Hull Numbers, Builders and Key Dates

Aircraft Carrier

		Builder	Originally Commissioned	Finally Paid Off	Disposal
22	Bonaventure	HW	17/01/57	01/07/70	broken up (b.u.) Formosa, 1970

Cruisers

31	Quebec	VN	21/10/44	13/06/56	b.u. Osaka, Japan, 1961
32	Ontario	HW	16/04/45	15/10/58	b.u. Osaka, Japan, 1960

Tribal Class Destroyers

				Finally Paid Off	Disposal
213	Nootka	HX	07/08/46	06/02/64	b.u. Faslane, Scotland, 1965
214	Micmac	HX	12/09/45	31/03/64	b.u. Faslane, Scotland, 1965
215	Haida	VN	30/08/43	11/10/63	Ontario Place, 1970
216	Huron	VN	19/07/43	30/04/63	b.u. La Spezia, Italy, 1965
217	Iroquois	VN	30/11/42	24/10/62	b.u. Bilbao, Spain, 1966
218	Cayuga	HX	20/10/47	27/02/64	b.u. Faslane, Scotland, 1965
219	Athabaskan	HX	20/01/48	21/04/66	b.u. La Spezia, Italy, 1970

"V" Class Destroyers

				Re-commissioned after conversion	Finally Paid Off	Disposal
224	Algonquin	JB	07/02/44	25/02/53	01/04/70	b.u. Taiwan, 1971
225	Sioux	WH	21/02/44		10/10/63	b.u. La Spezia, Italy, 1965

"C" Class Destroyers

226	Crescent	JB	10/09/45	1956	01/04/70	b.u. Taiwan, 1971
228	Crusader	JB	15/11/45		15/01/60	Sold for scrap, 1963

Prestonian Class Frigates

				Re-commissioned as Prestonian	Finally Paid Off	Disposal
304	New Waterford	YA	21/01/44	31/01/58	22/12/66	b.u. Savona, Italy, 1967
305	La Hulloise	CV	20/05/44	09/10/57	16/07/65	b.u. La Spezia, Italy, 1966
306	Swansea	YA	04/10/43	14/11/57	14/10/66	b.u. Savona, Italy, 1967
307	Prestonian	DS	13/09/44	22/08/53	24/04/56	Norwegian Navy, discarded 1972
308	Inch Arran	DS	18/11/44	23/08/54	23/06/65	scrapped 1970
310	Outremont	MO	27/11/43	02/09/55	07/06/65	b.u. La Spezia, Italy, 1966
312	Fort Erie	GD	27/10/44	17/04/56	26/03/65	b.u. La Spezia, Italy, 1966
314	Buckingham	DS	02/11/44	25/06/54	23/03/65	b.u. La Spezia, Italy, 1966
316	Penetang	DS	19/10/44	01/06/54	25/01/56	Norwegian Navy, then b.u. 1966
317	Cap de la Madeleine	MO	30/09/44	07/12/54	15/05/65	b.u. La Spezia, Italy, 1966
319	Toronto	DS	06/05/44	26/11/53	14/04/56	Norwegian Navy, discarded 1977
320	Victoriaville	GD	11/11/44	25/09/59	31/12/73	sold for scrap, 1974
321	Lanark	CV	06/07/44	15/04/56	19/03/65	b.u. La Spezia, Italy, 1966
322	Lauzon	GD	30/08/44	12/12/53	24/05/63	sold for scrap, 1964

Prestonian Class Frigates - fitted with cadet training gunroom

301	Antigonish	YA	04/07/44	12/10/57	30/11/66	b.u. Japan, 1968
303	Beacon Hill	YA	16/05/44	21/12/57	15/09/67	b.u. Sakai, Japan, 1968
309	Ste Thérèse	DS	28/05/44	21/01/55	30/01/67	b.u. Japan, 1967
311	Stettler	CV	07/05/44	27/02/54	31/08/66	b.u. Victoria, B.C., 1967
313	Sussexvale	DS	29/11/44	08/01/55	30/11/66	b.u. Japan, 1967
315	New Glasgow	YA	23/12/43	30/01/54	30/01/67	b.u. Japan, 1967
318	Jonquière	DS	10/05/44	20/09/54	23/09/66	b.u. Victoria, B.C., 1967

Bay Class Minesweepers

		Builder	Originally Commissioned	Finally Paid Off	Disposal
143	Gaspé	DS	05/12/53	22/08/57	To Turkish Navy
146	Comox	VM	02/04/54	11/09/57	To Turkish Navy
148	Ungava	DS	04/06/54	23/08/57	To Turkish Navy
149	Quinte	PA	15/10/54	26/02/64	Declared surplus, 1965
151	Fortune	VM	03/11/54	28/02/64	Sold for commercial purposes
152	James Bay	YA	03/05/54	28/02/64	Sold for use in under-sea oil exploration
154	Resolute	KI	16/09/54	14/02/64	Declared surplus, 1965
157	Trinity	GD	16/06/54	21/08/57	To Turkish Navy
159	Fundy	DS	27/11/56	19/12/96	sold to US interests, not to be scrapped
160	Chignecto	GD	01/08/57	19/12/96	sold to Canadian, for salvage and scrap
161	Thunder	PA	03/10/57	22/08/97	sold to US interests, not to be scrapped
162	Cowichan	YA	12/12/57	22/08/97	sold to US interests, not to be scrapped
163	Miramichi	VM	29/10/57	18/12/98	awaiting disposal, Esquimalt, B.C
164	Chaleur	MI	12/09/57	18/12/98	awaiting disposal, Esquimalt, B.C.

Escort Maintenance Ships

100	Cape Breton	BU	31/01/53	10/02/64	awaiting disposal, Esquimalt, B.C.
101	Cape Scott	BU	28/01/59	01/07/70	b.u. Texas, 1978

Gate Vessels

180	Porte St Jean	GD	05/12/51	29/03/96	sold to Halifax, N.S. interests, not to be scrapped
183	Porte St Louis	GD	29/08/52	29/03/96	sold to Halifax, N.S. interests, not to be scrapped
184	Porte de la Reine	VM	07/11/52	19/12/96	sold to Tacoma, Wash. interests, not to be scrapped
185	Porte Quebec	BU	19/09/52	19/12/96	sold to Tacoma, Wash. interests, not to be scrapped
186	Porte Dauphine	PF	10/12/52	see note	now "Salmon Harvester", in Queen Charlotte Islands. (Never officially paid off)

Canadian Warships

St Laurent Class Destroyer Escorts   Originally DDE, then DDH

			Re-comm'd as DDH	Finally Paid Off	Disposal
205	St. Laurent	CV	29/10/55	04/10/63	14/06/74	Sank off C. Hatteras, 1980
206	Saguenay	HX	15/12/56	14/05/65	26/06/90	Sunk 25/06/94 off Lunenburg, N.S.
207	Skeena	BU	30/03/57	14/08/65	01/11/93	b.u. India
229	Ottawa	CV	10/11/56	21/10/64	31/07/92	b.u. India
230	Margaree	HX	05/10/57	15/10/65	02/05/92	b.u. India
233	Fraser	BU	28/06/57	22/10/66	05/10/94	museum, Bridgewater, N.S.
234	Assiniboine	MI	16/08/56	28/06/63	14/12/88	scrapped, 1995

Restigouche Class Destroyer Escorts - DDE

				Re-commissioned after Major Refit DELEX	Finally Paid Off	Disposal
235	Chaudiere	HX	14/11/59		23/05/74		Sunk 14/06/97 Sechelt Inlet, B.C.
236	Gatineau	DS	17/02/59	14/04/71	12/11/82	24/05/96	awaiting disposal, Halifax, N.S.
256	St. Croix	MI	04/10/58			15/11/74	b.u. Virginia, USA
257	Restigouche	CV	07/06/58	1972	29/11/85	31/08/94	both 257 and 258 sold, and
258	Kootenay	BU	07/03/59	07/01/72	21/10/83	18/11/95	likely to be scrapped in China.
259	Terra Nova	VM	06/06/59	1986	09/11/84	11/07/97	awaiting disposal, Halifax, N.S.
260	Columbia	BU	07/11/59			18/02/74	Sunk 22/06/96 Maud Island, B.C.

Mackenzie Class Destroyer Escorts - DDE

261	Mackenzie	CV	06/10/62	1986-87	03/08/93	Sunk 15/09/95 Gooch Island, B.C.
262	Saskatchewan	VM	16/02/63	1985-86	28/03/94	Sunk 14/06/97 near Nanaimo, B.C.
263	Yukon	BU	25/05/63	1984-85	03/12/93	to be artificial reef off San Diego.
264	Qu'Appelle	DS	14/09/63	1983-84	31/07/92	sold for scrap

Annapolis Class Destroyer Escorts -DDH

265	Annapolis	HX	19/12/64	1985-86	18/07/98	awaiting disposal, Esquimalt, B.C.
266	Nipigon	MI	30/05/64	1983-84	03/07/98	awaiting disposal, Halifax, N.S.

Fast Hydrofoil Escorts

			Originally Comm'd	Finally Paid Off	Disposal
400	Bras d'Or	MI	18/07/68	01/05/72	Museum at L'Islet-sur-Mer, Quebec

Former USN Submarines

71	Grilse	Electric Boat, Groton	11/05/61	02/10/69	Returned to US Navy
75	Rainbow	Portsmouth, N.H.	02/12/68	31/12/74	b.u. Portland, Oregon

"O" Class Submarines

72	Ojibwa	all HM	23/09/65	21/05/98	awaiting disposal, Halifax, N.S.
73	Onondaga	Dockyard,	22/06/67		
74	Okanagan	Chatham	22/06/68	08/09/98	awaiting disposal, Halifax, N.S.

Operational Support Ships

		Builder	Originally Commissioned	Finally Paid Off	Disposal
508	Provider	DS	28/09/63	24/06/98.	Laid up, Halifax, NS
509	Protecteur	SJ	30/08/69		
510	Preserver	SJ	30/07/70		

Iroquois Class Destroyer Escorts - DDH

				TRUMP Major Refit
280	Iroquois	MI	29/07/72	1992
281	Huron	MI	16/12/72	1994
282	Athabaskan	DS	30/09/72	1994
283	Algonquin	DS	03/11/73	1991

Canadian Patrol Frigates

330	Halifax	SJ	29/06/92
331	Vancouver	SJ	23/08/93
332	Ville de Québec	MI	14/07/94
333	Toronto	SJ	19/07/93
334	Regina	MI	30/09/94
335	Calgary	MI	12/05/95
336	Montreal	SJ	21/07/94
337	Fredericton	SJ	10/09/94
338	Winnipeg	SJ	23/06/95
339	Charlottetown	SJ	09/09/95
340	St. John's	SJ	24/06/96
341	Ottawa	SJ	28/09/96

Kingston Class Maritime Coastal Defence Vessels

700	Kingston	HX	21/09/96
701	Glace Bay	HX	26/10/96
702	Nanaimo	HX	10/05/97
703	Edmonton	HX	21/06/97
704	Shawinigan	HX	14/06/97
705	Whitehorse	HX	17/04/98
706	Yellowknife	HX	18/04/98
707	Goose Bay	HX	26/07/98
708	Moncton	HX	12/07/98
709	Saskatoon	HX	05/12/98
710	Brandon	HX	05/06/99 (scheduled)
711	Summerside	HX	18/07/99 (scheduled)

Minesweeping Auxiliaries

110	Anticosti	AS	07/05/89
112	Moresby	AS	07/05/89

Diving Support Vessel

			Finally Paid Off
20	Cormorant	10/11/78	02/07/97.	Sold to US Interests, to continue in diving support.

Key to Builders' Abbreviations

- AS Allied Shipbuilding, Vancouver, B.C.
- BU Burrard Dry Dock Co. Ltd., Vancouver, B.C.
- CV Canadian Vickers Ltd., Montreal, Quebec
- DS Davie Shipbuilding and Repairing Co. Ltd., Lauzon, Quebec
- GD George T. Davie & Sons Ltd., Lauzon, Quebec
- HW Harland & Wolff Ltd., Belfast, Northern Ireland
- HX Halifax Shipyards Ltd., Halifax, N.S.
- JB   John Brown & Co. Ltd., Glasgow, Scotland
- KI   Kingston Shipbuilding Co. Ltd., Kingston, Ont.
- MI   Marine Industries Ltd., Sorel, Quebec
- MO Morton Engineering and Dry Dock Co., Quebec City, Quebec
- PA Port Arthur Shipbuilding Co. Ltd., Port Arthur, Ont.
- PF   Pictou Foundry Co., Pictou, N.S.
- SJ   Saint John Dry Dock and Shipbuilding Co. Ltd., Saint John, N.B.
- VM Victoria Machinery Depot Co. Ltd., Victoria, B.C.
- VN Vickers-Armstrong Ltd., Newcastle-on-Tyne, England.
- WH J. Samuel White & Co., Ltd., Cowes, Isle of Wight, England
- YA Yarrows Ltd., Esquimalt, B.C.

Appendix B:
Recollections of Command of Three Ships

The *Restigouche* class DDE, HMCS *Terra Nova* shows her forefoot while fuelling from *Provider*, in this photograph from Vice Admiral (Ret'd) J.A. Fulton, then commanding officer of *Provider*. During this evolution Fulton signaled to *Terra Nova*, "You are showing your forefoot". *Terra Nova* replied "Don't laugh. So are you from time to time!" Her 3-inch-70 gun turret is trained aft, to protect its barrels and gun layer's plexiglass window from the heavy seas. Fulton relates:

I had the honour to command three of Her Majesty's Canadian ships—*Outremont*, *Gatineau* and *Provider*. Each ship was different and each posed a challenge to me.

In *Outremont* I discovered that workups and general seamanship were essential and highly necessary to be a good fleet unit. An East German freighter was disabled in a severe Atlantic storm and *Outremont* took the ship in tow and towed it 200 miles to Halifax.

Gatineau was almost new in 1965—just broken in you might say. In her we perfected our operational skills in ASW. *Gatineau* and *Columbia* had a most thrilling encounter with an RN submarine. After 45 minutes of hot pursuit the submarine surfaced, out of battery.

Provider was almost new, like *Gatineau*, and a very different challenge. In my three years in command we did many fleet replenishments. Some of these were very exciting as these pictures of *Terra Nova* show fairly well. On the West Coast there were no Canadian Navy helicopters. We were fortunate to get USN Sea King helicopters to operate from our deck in all major international exercises conducted in 1969-72. During that time we followed a Russian naval squadron from Alaska to Hawaii and in the many joint exercises our USN helicopters were credited with two USN submarines which was two more than anyone else could claim.

They were all great ships and their crews were outstanding. I am sure each Captain, if asked, would tell a similar story with the same pride.

by Vice Admiral J.A. Fulton, Ret'd

Appendix C:
An Officer-of-the-Watch's Impression of Driving a Halifax Class CPF

by SLt G. R. Steed

To give an Officer-of-the-Watch's impression of the exhilaration of "driving" Canada's newest frigates, I would like to describe the occasion in which manoeuvering the ship is most critical. This is during replenishment at sea (RAS). This is perhaps one of the most dangerous operations conducted by warships in peacetime. It involves bringing fast-moving ships together until they are steaming on parallel courses only 80 feet apart. I grant you, 80 feet on the highway is a lot of room, but when bringing 4,500 tons of ship alongside another of equal or greater size at between 15 and 30 knots, there is not much room for error. So why do it? Simply because performing it is essential if ships are to remain on station without needing to enter port to fuel or replenish supplies.

How is this accomplished? Normally 30 minutes prior to a RAS, the appropriate personnel are closed up to carry out the evolution, and the machinery configuration altered to assume the 2 gas-turbine cross-connected (2GT X-Con) drive-mode, as this offers the greatest redundancy for propulsion and speed. The Officer-of-the-Watch (OOW) has the responsibility for proper and safe movement and operation of the ship, as well as for the safety of the ship's company. This means that he is responsible for conning the ship, adjusting course and speed, as well as supervision of all personnel of the watch-on-deck, receiving reports and giving direction to the engineering OOW and the operations room.

The manouevre most often conducted is known as "joining from ahead." Picture, if you will, two ships steaming almost directly towards each other, on essentially collision courses, at a combined speed of 35 to 40 knots and you will realize that things happen very quickly. The OOW and his team use a number of tools including a problem solving technique known as relative velocity, to figure out how to get into station, knowing the advance and transfer of the ship at a given speed, as well as her acceleration and deceleration characteristics. The object of the exercise is to get into your station, six degrees off the tanker, or guide ship's stern, at a range of 500 yards and 150 feet displaced from the guide's wake, without colliding with the guide. This involves executing a precisely timed sharp U-turn. Turn too soon, and you'll make a sizeable hole in the tanker. Turn too late, and you'll spend the next 15 minutes trying to catch up with her. With enough practice, an experienced OOW is capable of getting into station with a minimum of helm orders, with an error of less than 50 yards or 2 degrees of bearing. Once in station, the next part of the operation is to "drive" into the RAS position alongside the tanker. Essentially this involves putting on speed and "driving" forward to come abreast of the tanker, which has been happily steaming a steady course at typically 15 knots throughout all this excitement, but not necessarily. However, acceleration and deceleration play a role, as it is important not to shoot through your station. The last part of this operation is to remain in station while the fuelling hoses are passed across. This is perhaps the easiest part of the entire operation, as one makes speed and course adjustments to keep even with the tanker in order that lines and fuelling hoses may be passed between the two ships, and refuelling safely conducted.

Mere words are completely inadequate to convey the excitement of this manoeuvre, with the wind whistling through the rigging, and the spray from the bow wave blowing over the fo'c'sle and the bridge. It takes a pretty cool commanding officer to stand back and watch a young officer-of-the-watch con his ship through such an approach, without intervening and taking charge himself!

Appendix D:
Astro Navigation: An Explanation

The author is seen as an acting sub-lieutenant "shooting the sun", on the flag deck of *Chaudière*, while in mid-Atlantic, returning to Halifax from Londonderry in the summer of 1963 with the Fifth Canadian Escort Squadron. Astro navigation, using the heavenly bodies to "fix" a ship's position, is little used now, in this age of satellite global positioning systems, but at that time it was essential, once out of range of land and radio aids to navigation such as Decca and Loran.

The sextant is a precision optical instrument used to measure the height above the horizon of a heavenly body, typically a star or the sun. One uses the measured heights above the horizon of several heavenly bodies in a calculation to work out the ship's position.

The officer-of-the-watch of a ship at sea should always keep up the ship's "DR", the "dead reckoning" track of the ship, plotting where the ship should be, based on how long the ship has steamed in a particular direction at a particular speed since the last time he "got a fix", or fixed the ship's position. In this way, even when there's "no moon, no stars, November", he always has some idea of where the ship is.

However, the ship's DR position can be used to calculate the heights various heavenly bodies would be above the horizon at the time of one's sight if the ship really was exactly at the DR position at that exact time. One then subtracts the sextant-measured heights from the calculated heights, the differences being how far the ship is from where one thought it was, on lines pointing towards or away from the heavenly bodies one was "shooting". The ship is then somewhere on a position line at right angles to the line pointing towards each heavenly body concerned. The intersection of these position lines is the position of the ship at the time of the sight. With care, three or four position lines intersect in a single point, or at worst, they form a "cocked hat" only a nautical mile or two across.

For this to work at all, one needs to be able to see both the horizon, and some stars or the sun. One can therefore "shoot" morning and evening stars during morning and evening twilight, respectively, and, during the day, "shoot" typically two suns in the morning, and two in the afternoon, these being termed "sun-run-suns", as well as the sun's meridian passage, or "merpass", when the sun is due south, on the meridian, which will very easily give one's latitude. All weather permitting, of course! One also needs to know, quite accurately, the time one shot each star or sun, so an assistant stands by with a deck watch and notebook to record the precise time of each sextant measurement. In this way, one will have obtained as many as seven "fixes" through the day, morning stars, the morning sun-run-sun, merpass, the afternoon sun-run-sun, and evening stars. Because one cannot see the horizon during the night, one can only use dead reckoning to estimate the ship's position through the night.

Taking morning or evening stars takes perhaps 15 minutes' preparation so that one will know which star one is shooting, and as much as three quarters of an hour's calculation and plotting afterwards to deduce one's position, or to be exact, one's position when one actually took the sight. However, when one is out of sight of land, steaming at, say, 15 knots, it is quite acceptable to take 45 minutes to work out where one was 45 minutes ago, as one's ship will only have steamed 11¼ nautical miles in that time interval! And one doesn't need satellites, which would likely be disabled in wartime. In case you are wondering, one could and did use the visible planets as well as the stars, but the moon was very seldom used as it usually gave quite inaccurate results.

Air navigators, incidentally, used to use a bubble sextant, to give an artificial horizon, so they could shoot stars at any time of the night. And with so called rapid sight reduction tables, they could compute their position in very much less than 45 minutes.

Appendix E:
Anchoring a Warship:
It's More Than Just Dropping the Hook!

Cdr. W.G. Kinsman, commanding officer, and the author as navigator in the starboard bridge wing of *Gatineau* anchor the ship off Dark Island in the St. Lawrence River, some ten miles upstream of Brockville, Ontario, in the summer of 1965. Lt. A.J. Walzak is "in the chains", as fo'c'sle officer. I am taking cut-off bearings, sighting over the gyro compass repeater, to inform the captain how many cables to go to the anchor letting-go position. The group in the starboard bridge wing consists of, left to right, a seaman with headphones in touch with the cable party on the fo'c'sle, Cdr. Kinsman, the Chief Yeoman of Signals standing directly in front of the 10-inch signal lamp, my Navigator's Yeoman Able Seaman Ford, the author, and the executive officer, LCdr Gerry Hill.

The captain will lower the green anchor flag he is holding when I, as navigator call "Let go now, please, Sir", green to indicate that the starboard anchor is to be used. The fo'c'sle officer, seeing the captain's anchor flag fall, will give the order to the fo'c'sle party, in the cable deck below the fo'c'sle, to let the anchor go, either by knocking off the slip which is holding the anchor cable, or by taking off the brake on the cable windlass. From his position in the chains, a platform only rigged for anchoring, he will be able to see and report to the bridge the direction the anchor cable is leading away from the ship. He will give reports such as "cable long stay forward", "cable up and down", and "ship has got her cable," this last report when the cable has jerked taut, and then relaxed, indicating that the anchor is holding. Equally important, but not visible in the picture, the special-sea-duty-officer-of-the-watch is in the bridge conning the ship along the track I, as navigator, have requested to the anchor letting go position.

However, dropping the anchor in the right place is not the end of the story. The officer-of-the-watch will continue to ensure that the ship remains within a circle of radius equal to the amount of cable paid out, with centre at the letting go position, until it is time to weigh anchor and proceed, either taking visual or radar fixes at frequent intervals.

Anchors and their chain cables are very heavy, and an inattentive cable party could easily allow the anchor cable to run out until pulled up short by the cable clench in the bottom of the cable locker. Allowing the inner end of the ship's anchor cable to disappear into the water, leaving the ship drifting freely, was not recommended! However, an anchor buoy, attached by a line to the anchor before letting go, would give some chance of finding the anchor in the mud on the bottom.

Other details visible in the picture are the doorway into the bridge, and the pre-wetting piping around the forward edge of the bridge structure, used to wet down the superstructure before steaming through a radioactive cloud. A whip antenna parallels the right hand edge of the picture, just to the right of the bridge wing.

Appendix F:
Ordering Engine Movements, and Steam Turbine Propulsion

This is the manoeuvering platform in the engine room of the *Restigouche* class DDE, *Chaudière*. The starboard engine's throttle valve handwheels are on the left, the port on the right, the larger wheel being for the ahead turbine throttle, and the smaller wheel for the astern turbine. "Slow Ahead Starboard, Half Astern Port!". Today's ships have direct hands-on control levers on the bridge for the engines, but in earlier ships such as this the officer-of-the-watch would give his engine orders to the quartermaster in the wheelhouse by microphone or voicepipe. There the bosun's mate would relay the orders from the wheelhouse to the engine room by engine room telegraphs, and the engine room watchkeeper would execute those orders by manipulating the engine throttles. This process was particularly critical when bringing a ship alongside a jetty in harbour, when engine revolutions and direction were sometimes altered many times in a few minutes.

In the "steamers", before the days of gas turbines and controllable pitch propellers, it was the custom to order engine movements and ship's speed by the orders stop, slow, half, and full ahead or astern, port, starboard, or both engines. Slow meant a defined number of engine revolutions per minute, and half ahead meant operating the engines at the particular number of revolutions ordered, for example, "Revolutions one-four-zero", i.e. 140 revolutions per minute. And at the end of the hour, after steaming at 140 revolutions, for example, the rev counters of each shaft had to show an increase of 140 x 60 = 8400 revolutions. Occasionally the officer-of-the-watch would have cause to wonder whether engine room watchkeepers were getting a little enthusiastic, making up their turn count to compensate for having run too slowly earlier in the hour. The frustration of crossing the Atlantic from Londonderry to Halifax in August 1963 at economical speed, 15 knots, caused one wag to break into verse:-

We are all headed west, at economy best,
For days at this speed we have floated.
I've just been advised, though it's not advertised,
That homeward-bound turns won't be noted!

The more technically curious reader may be interested to know that each of the two Babcock and Wilcox - Goldie McCullough boilers of the St Laurent, Restigouche, Mackenzie, and Annapolis class ships produced a maximum of 135,000 lbs/hour of superheated steam at 37.92 bar (550 psi) and 454°C (850°F), from 235°F feedwater, by burning 10,920 lbs/hour of fuel oil. This was fed to two high pressure turbines, one driving each shaft. Each turbine had eight ahead impulse stages and an astern two-row standard Curtis wheel. The design output from each turbine was 15,000 shp full ahead, and 4,300 shp full astern, giving 225 and 150 rpm of the propeller shafts respectively. Ahead turbine rotor speed at full power was 5,750 rpm. If memory serves, the reduction ratio of the main gearing was 25:1.

One of the turbines of *Algonquin* is shown opened up for inspection during her major refit in 1964-1965 in Marine Industries Limited, Sorel. The half joints of both her low pressure turbines were broken, each upper casing laboriously raised on four jack screws to expose its blading, and the rotor of each turbine then lifted in the same way to expose the lower casing half's blading. The reaction forces from the steam flowing between the fixed and moving rows of blades convert the thermal energy of the steam into the mechanical energy of the rotating shaft.

In passing through the high and low pressure turbines, the superheated steam will expand from a pressure of as much as 400 pounds per square inch (psi) all the way down to 29 inches of mercury vacuum, depending upon the temperature of the seawater flowing through the condenser tubes. The water formed in the condensers is sucked out by the condensate extraction pumps, passed through the de-aerator, and pumped back to the boilers by the boiler feed pumps.

It is worth pointing out that steam enters the low pressure turbine, seen in the photograph, between the two shortest stages of blading, and flows outwards towards both ends of the turbine rotor, through successively longer blades, losing pressure and temperature, until it leaves the turbine altogether and flows into the underslung condenser. Nearest the lefthand end of the rotor are three rows of Curtis blading which form the astern turbine. Steam admitted to this blading will turn the rotor in the opposite direction.

Appendix G:
Gas Turbine Marine Propulsion

The marine gas turbine is now quite widely used, having displaced the steam turbine to a large extent in small and medium sized surface warships. The General Electric LM2500 gas turbine which powers the *Halifax* Class Patrol Frigate has seen service in well over 330 ships in 24 navies of the free world, first going into service in 1969.

Essentially the engine is a conventional jet engine with a power turbine coupled on the back to convert the energy of the high temperature exhaust gases into the mechanical energy of a rotating shaft.

The LM2500 marine gas turbine is a simple-cycle, two-shaft, high-performance engine. From left to right in the drawing, it is composed of four major components:

- a 16-stage compressor — 18:1 pressure ratio, first 7 stages featuring variable stators and inlet guide vanes, enabling easy starting, good part-load performance, high efficiency, and high stall margin over the entire operating range;

- a fully annular combustor — externally mounted fuel nozzles support liquid fuel combustion; assures virtually smokeless operation through the complete power range, even while burning heavy distillate fuels:

- a 2-stage high-pressure turbine — air-cooled for long life, drives the compressor and accessory drive gearbox;

- the 6-stage low-pressure power turbine, aerodynamically coupled to the gas generator, driven by the gas generator's high energy release exhaust flow.

-with information from GE Marine and Industrial Engines' booklet, *LM2500: Unparalleled Marine Power*

"Stage" here refers to any two adjacent rows of blading, one moving, secured to a rotor, and the other fixed, secured to the stator. Not shown in the drawing, the power turbine is coupled through flexible couplings, connected to the power turbine driving flange at extreme right, to one of the ship's main reduction gearboxes. Mounted underneath the compressor is the accessory gearbox, at the after end of which is mounted the oil hydraulically driven starter motor.

Air is drawn into the axial-flow compressor through the bell-shaped intake structure at left, and raised to an approximate temperature and pressure of 1260°F and 260psi. Fuel is continuously injected into the annular combustion chamber, and the resulting hot gases first pass through the high pressure turbine blading, driving the compressor on the same shaft, and then the power turbine, on its own separate shaft, emerging with an exhaust gas temperature of 1051°F. The compressor/high pressure turbine, or gas generator, shaft, has an idle speed of 4900-5000rpm, and a maximum speed of 9800rpm. The power turbine has a maximum speed of 3600rpm, and is not normally driven at lower than 600rpm, due to torque limitations. The gas turbines fitted in the Halifax Class Patrol Frigate are rated at 17.7MW (sustained), or 23,727hp.

The beauty of modern gas turbines is that they can be brought from "cold iron" up to idle speed, and access to full power, in a mere 90 seconds. The starter motor runs up the gas generator spool to a light-off speed of around 1200rpm, at which time fuel admission is commenced, using spark igniters, as the compressor outlet temperature at that speed is insufficient to support combustion. The igniters are turned off just prior to the gas generator reaching idle speed of 4900-5000rpm, and are not required during normal operation.

The gas turbines in the *Halifax* Class were built in the late eighties. Several improvements have been made since then, significantly increasing the engine's rating. The specifications of today's LM2500 Gas Turbine currently quoted by General Electric have been added to the cutaway drawing, reproduced with permission.

Nominal Continuous Power		33,600 (bhp)
59°F, Zero Losses		25,060 (kW)
Specific Fuel Consumption	(lb/bhp-hr)	0.373
	(g/bhp-hr)	169.3
Exhaust Gas Flow	(lb/sec)	155
	(kg/sec)	70.4
Exhaust Gas Temperature	(°F)	1,051
	(°C)	566
Output Speed (rpm)		3,600
Dimensions, L/W/H	(inches)	257/82/80
	(mm)	6,528/2,083/2,042
Engine Weight	(lb)	10,300
	(kg)	4,676

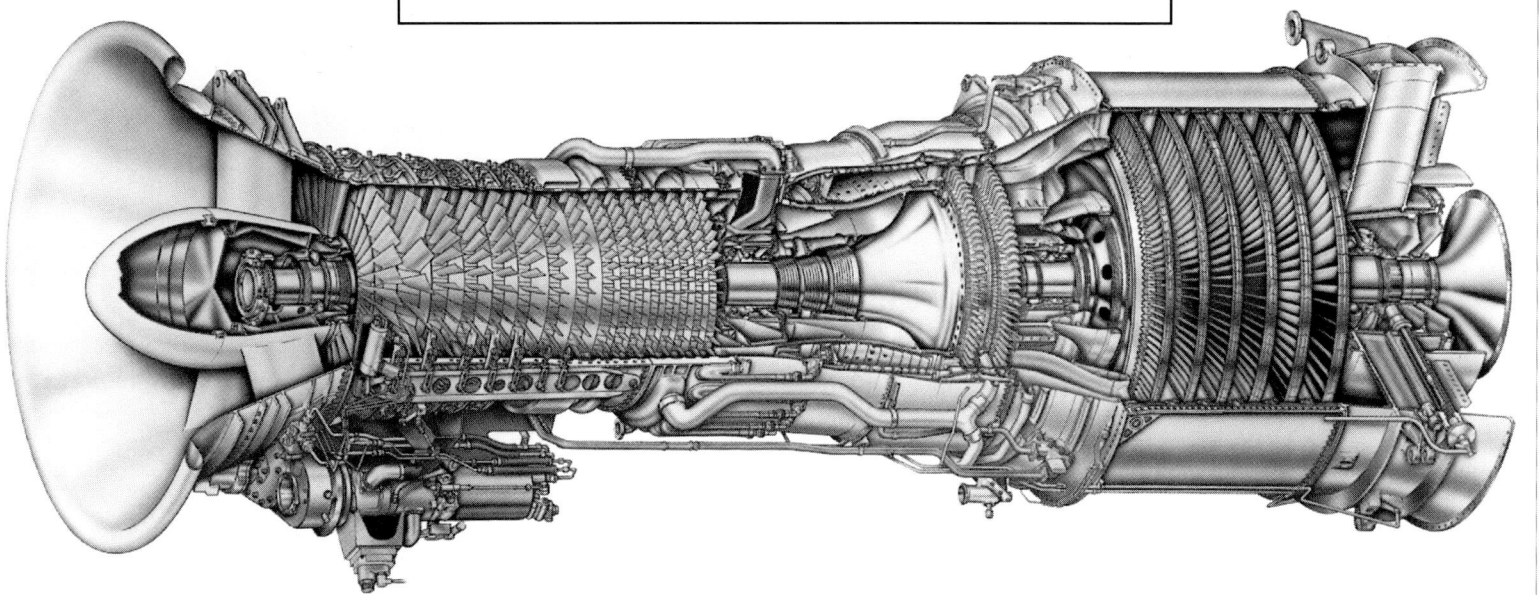

Cutaway Drawing of the General Electric LM2500 Gas Turbine

BIBLIOGRAPHY

Critchley, Michael. *The Royal Navy in Focus, 1960-1969*. Cornwall: Maritime Books, 1992.

Ferguson, Julie. *Through a Canadian Periscope: The Story of the Canadian Submarine Service*. Hamilton: Dundurn Press, 1995.

Geneja, Stephen Conrad. *The Cruiser Uganda: One War, Many Conflicts*. Corbyville, ON: Tyendinaga Publishers, 1994.

Johnson, Richard C. *Antenna Engineering Handbook*. Third Edition. New York: McGraw Hill, 1993.

Lynch, Thomas G. *The Flying 400: Canada's Hydrofoil Project*. Halifax, NS: Nimbus Publishing, 1983.

Lynch, Thomas G. "Eliminating 'Hot-Spots': Canadian Naval IR Suppression Systems." *Navy International* (May 1992), 119-123.

Macpherson, Ken and Ron Barrie. *Cadillac of Destroyers: HMCS St. Laurent and her Successors*. St. Catharines: Vanwell Publishing Ltd, 1996.

Macpherson, Ken, and John Burgess. *The Ships of Canada's Naval Forces 1910-1993*. St. Catharines, ON: Vanwell Publishing Ltd, 1994.

Schull, Joseph. *Far Distant Ships: An Official Account of Canadian Naval Operations in World War II*. Toronto: Stoddart Publishing Ltd, 1989.

Shadwick, Martin. "The Canadian Navy: A Search for Relevance." *The Naval Balance 1990*, No. 11 Vol XI. Naval Forces: International Forum for Maritime Power. Bonn: Mönch Publishing Group, 1990, 21-27.

Snowie, J. Allan. *The Bonnie: HMCS Bonaventure*. Erin, ON: Boston Mills Press, 1987.

Spicer, the Hon. Sir John. "Report of the Royal Commission on the Loss of HMAS *Voyager*. Commonwealth of Australia, 1964.

_____. Admiralty Manual of Navigation. Vol I-III. London: HMSO, 1959.

_____. *Canada's Navy Annual*, No.1-6. Special Ed,. *Wings* Magazine. Calgary: Corvus Publishing Group Ltd., 1986 to 1992.

_____. *Jane's All the World's Aircraft.* Surrey, UK: Jane's Information Group Ltd, 1998.

_____. *Jane's Fighting Ships*. Surrey, UK: Jane's Information Group Ltd, 1998.

_____. *LM2500 - Unparalleled Marine Power.* GE Marine & Industrial Engines. Cincinnati, Ohio. 1995.

_____. *Manual of Seamanship* Vol I-III. London: HMSO, 1951.

_____. *Saint John Shipbuilding, Canada*. Special Supplement of Naval Forces: International Forum for Maritime Power. Bonn: Mönch Publishing Group, 1993.

INTERNET WEBSITES

Artificial Reef Society of British Columbia. http://www.artificialreef.bc.ca/. January 31, 1999.

Proc, Jerry. ASDIC, RADAR and IFF Systems Aboard HMCS Haida. http://webhome.idirect.com/~jproc/sari/sarintro.html. January 31, 1999.

Canada's Navy on the West Coast. http://www.dnd.ca/navy/marpac/site1/homepage.htm. January 31, 1999.

Canadian Navy of Yesterday and Today, by Sandy McClearn. http://www.uss-salem.org/navhist/canada/. January 31, 1999.

General Electric Marine Gas Turbines. http://www.ge.com/aircraftengines/marine/mspecs.htm#LM2500. January 31, 1999.

HMCS *Haida* Naval Museum. http://www3.sympatico.ca/hrc/haida/home.htm. January 31, 1999.

Jane's Defence. http://www.janes.com/defence/defset.html. January 31, 1999.

Maritime Forces Atlantic Fleet. http://www.marlant.hlfx.dnd.ca/marlant/mar002e.html. January 31, 1999.

INDEX

Aircraft carriers 9, 38

Anchoring 85

Argus aircraft 20

Astro navigation 84

Bathythermograph 21

Bay class minesweepers 68, 69

Bear trap 49, 54

Budge, RAdm P.D. 13

Canadian Patrol Frigates 57-60, 82

Cruisers 11, 12, 13

Destroyer escorts 10, 15-17, 23, 29

DDEs 29, 31, 32, 35, 37, 40, 43-46

DDHs 30, 41, 47, 50

Falls, Adm R.H. . . . . .v, 33

Fleck, Cdr Laverne 60

Frigates 24-28

Gas turbines 36, 50, 52, 56, 57, 61, 88

Harpoon missile . . . . .ii, 57

Halifax class, driving 60

HU-21 HO4S-3 Helicopter "Pedro" 9, 42

Hydrofoil 36

Improved *Restigouche* class 35, 37, 43-46, 75

Infra-red signatures 56, 57

Jackstay Transfer 26

Joining from ahead 82

Kinsman, Cdr W.G. 85

Limbo 21, 42

Mackenzie class 40

Maritime Coastal Defence Vessels 72

Minesweepers 68, 69

Modern marine radars 34

Nixon, Capt C.P. 33

Oberon class submarines 66

Plane guard destroyer 9

Porter, VAdm. H.A. 26

Radar frequencies 18

Refuelling at Sea 10, 39

Restigouche class 30-32, 34, 37

Sea King helicopter 49, 54

Sea Sparrow missile 57, 59

Sonobuoys 9, 20

Squid 14, 16, 42

Steam turbines 87

Submarines 64-68

Tracker aircraft 9, 38

Tribal Class (original) 15, 16, 49

Tribal Class (2nd) 50-53

Trumped *Tribals* 55, 56, 63

Upholder class submarines 67, 68

Variable Depth Sonar (VDS) 14, 23, 47, 48, 51

YAGs 74